CW00361962

JO

OUR STORY

OUR STORY

by Reg and Ron Kray

with Fred Dinenage

SIDGWICK & JACKSON
LONDON

First published in September 1988 by Sidgwick and Jackson Limited

First Reprinted in September 1988

Second Reprint November 1988

Copyright © 1988 by Bejubop Limited

Pictures © 1988 by Bejubop Limited

All rights reserved. No part of this book may reproduced or transmitted in any form or by any means, electronic or mechanical, including photocopying, recording or by any information storage and retrieval system, without permission in writing from the publisher.

ISBN 0-283-99525-4

Typeset by Hewer Text Composition Services, Edinburgh

Printed by Mackays of Chatham PLC, Chatham, Kent
for Sidgwick & Jackson Limited
1 Tavistock Chambers, Bloomsbury Way
London WC1A 2SG

To our mother

Contents

Foreword

'I sentence you to life imprisonment, which I would recommend should not be less than thirty years.'

So said Mr Justice Melford Stevenson to the Kray twins, Reggie and Ronnie, at the Old Bailey, on 8 March 1969. They had been found guilty of the gangland killings of George Cornell and Jack 'The Hat' McVitie. The twins were thirty-four. At the time of the publication of this, their own story, they are fifty-four. They still, therefore, officially have ten years left to serve.

Most of Reggie Kray's twenty years in captivity have been spent as a Category A prisoner in the maximum-security Parkhurst prison near Newport on the Isle of Wight. At the time of writing he is at maximum-security Gartree prison near Market Harborough in Leicestershire. Despite repeated appeals he has been given no official indication that he will serve anything less than the thirty years to which he was sentenced.

His brother Ronnie began his sentence at Durham gaol, was then transferred to Parkhurst after a campaign led by the twins' mother, but has spent the last sixteen years at Broadmoor maximum-security psychiatric hospital near Crowthorne in Berkshire. He believes that he will never be released.

Fred Dinenage

ROYAL ALBERT HALL

Manager - - - C. S. TAYLOR

JACK CAPPELL PRESENTS AN INTERNATIONAL BOXING TOURNAMENT

TUESDAY, DECEMBER 11th 1951

Doors open 6.45.   Commence 7.30.   Matchmaker: JOHN S. SHARPE

10 (3-min.) Rounds International Lightweight Contest at 9.11

TOMMY McGOVERN

Lightweight Champion of Great Britain.   Versus

ALLAN TANNER

(British Guiana).   Sensationally defeated Ellis Ask, Tony Lombard

---

8 3-min. Rds. Welterweight at 10.10

JACKIE **BRADDOCK** v CHRISTIAN **CHRISTENSEN**

(Manchester)   (Denmark)

8 3-min. Rds. Bantamweight at 8.9

RON **JOHNSON** v JIMMY **CARDEW**

(Bethnal Green)   (Holloway)

---

8 3-min. Rds. Middleweight at 11.9

JIMMY **DAVIS** v JIMMY **JAMES**

(Bethnal Green)   (Trinidad)

6 3-min. Rds. Welterweight at 10.9

LEW **LAZAR** v CHARLIE **KRAY**

(Aldgate)   (Bethnal Green)

---

8 3-min. Rds. International Cruiserweight Contest at 12.10

JOHNNY McGOWAN v ERIC JENSEN

Central Area Champion   Light-heavyweight Champion of Denmark

---

6 3-min. Rds Lightweight Contest

REG **KRAY** v BOB **MANITO**

(Bethnal Green)   (Clapham)

6 3-min. Rds. Lightweight Contest

RON **KRAY** v BILL **SLINEY**

(Bethnal Green)   (Kings Cross)

Special Ringside **63/-**

PRICES: 42/- 30/- 21/- 15/- 10/6 5/- 2/6

Betting Strictly Prohibited   Rights of admission reserved

Tickets from: **PHIL COREN** (Box Office Manager) **GER 1742**
Jack Cappell Promotions (GER 1742-3-4) Royal Albert Hall (Ken 8212)

Reg: Introduction

I did not intend to tell this story, not until the day they finally release me. I have always believed that if I spoke out, if I told the true story of the Kray twins, it would count against me, that the authorities would make me serve every single day of the thirty years in prison to which I have been sentenced.

But then I received a letter from my brother Ron in Broadmoor. Ron and I have never lost touch. We write every day and every few months I'm taken to Broadmoor in an armoured truck to spend the day with him. Why the armoured truck, I don't know. After twenty years in captivity, I am not likely to do a bunk now.

Whenever we meet we spend the day talking. We don't talk about the past, we talk about the future. Ron and I have always believed we will be released one day. We have to believe it, it's all there is. We talk about the house we'll live in together in the country and about the places we want to see before we get too old. For years now we've talked about going to India and China, two of the most beautiful and interesting countries in the world. Every time I see Ron, that's all he really wants to talk about – how we'll go to India and China and what it will be like.

Then I got this letter from him – and it bloody nearly broke me up. Me, the man who was supposed to be the hard man of Parkhurst, the toughest con in the place. What it said was this:

Dear Reg,
    I have reason to believe I will never get out.
    I feel a bit sad tonight, as much as I have resigned myself to the fact

xi

that I won't be getting out. I would have loved to have come to India, China and all the other beautiful countries.

But I hope you will visit all these places, as that will compensate me, if you go instead. It will make me happy that one of us has been to all these places. Apart from this, I am very happy.

God bless
Ron

Those, to me, are the words of a man who has lost hope. After twenty years of trying, the system has finally crushed the spirit of my brother. That's why I now want to tell my side of the story, and why I want Ron to tell his.

I want society to know the true story of the terrible Kray twins, so that people can judge for themselves if we've paid the price. And if our punishment for telling this story is that we shall stay where we are, then what the hell? My brother believes he's never going to get out anyway, and I will continue to baffle the doctors and psychiatrists who say that fifteen years as a Category A prisoner will turn a man into a human vegetable. Well, I was Category A for seventeen years, and, believe me, I'm still as sharp as a razor.

And I will be when I get out – whether it's in one year or ten.

1

Memories of an East End Childhood

Reg: Born to Be Violent

I was born to be violent. When I was young most of my violence
happened in the boxing ring. I was good enough to have become a
great champion, but something happened to me when I was about
eight years old which, looking back, was an omen – a sign of the bad
things to come. That was when I was involved, for the first time, in
the death of another person.

I have never revealed this before. I have carried it around in my
heart and on my conscience for nearly fifty years, and it is something
that bothers me far more than any of my other crimes.

I was out one day with a streetwise little mate of mine called
Tommy, who lived just round the corner from me in Bethnal Green
in the East End of London. We were just out walking, mucking
about, looking for a bit of mischief to get up to. Remember, this was
London in the middle of war and Bethnal Green was one of the
poorest parts of the whole city. It was the kind of place where kids
were bound to get into bother every now and then. Tommy and I
were just larking about when he spotted an empty bread van parked
in the road. It was a typical road in that part of London: row after
row of depressing terraced houses, made worse by the German
bombing. It was a right dump. The driver of the van was delivering
his bread a bit farther up the street. Tommy gave me a nudge,
opened the door of the van and climbed in behind the steering wheel.
He whispered to me to get in the other side of the cab.

It was only a lark up to then, but Tommy noticed that the driver
had left the ignition keys in the van. 'We'll start the bugger up,' he
said. We weren't going to nick the van or anything like that. Tommy
was just going to start it up and then we'd bugger off a bit sharpish,
before the driver copped hold of us and gave us a bloody good hiding.

But Tommy didn't realize that the driver had left the gearstick in reverse. When he turned the ignition on, the van sort of jumped backwards. Not very far, but there was a bumping sound and a bloody terrifying scream. I swear, sometimes I can still hear that scream in my nightmares even now.

Tommy switched the ignition off and we both jumped out. We rushed to the back of the van and there was this little kid trapped between the back of the van and some rubble which had been left lying in the road – rubble caused by that bastard Hitler's bombs. I recognized the kid immediately. He had a twin sister and they lived quite close to us, just a couple of streets away. There was a lot of blood, the poor kid was bent into a peculiar shape and he wasn't moving. We knew straightaway he was either dead or very seriously injured. I know it's disgraceful, but Tommy and I did what most kids would have done in those circumstances, I suppose – we scarpered. We ran off as quick as our legs would take us. We were bloody horrified by what we'd done.

We heard later that the boy had died instantly. At least he hadn't been in pain for a long time. But for weeks we lived in fear that the coppers would come round looking for us and lock us up. Or the boy's father would come round and kill us for what we'd done. But no one ever did come for us. If anyone saw what had happened, and I'm sure someone must have, then they didn't want to get involved. No one ever named us as the killers.

They had an inquest later and the verdict was accidental death. They said the handbrake on the van must have slipped and the van rolled backwards, trapping the boy between the back of the van and the rubble. But I know different and I've had it on my mind ever since.

That little boy was the only innocent person either my brother Ron or I ever hurt in our whole lives. It wasn't completely my fault, it was just a stupid kids' game that went wrong. But if that boy's twin sister reads this – and she will know who I mean – I just want to say I'm sorry, really sorry. I wish now that I'd owned up at the time and faced the music. That, I suppose, was the first really black cloud to come over the life of Reggie Kray, though there have been a lot ever since.

I was born at eight o'clock at night on 24 October 1933, in Stene

2

Street, Hoxton, in London's East End. It's a depressing area of grey streets just outside the City, along the Hackney Road. Some of the poorest houses and people in England were to be found there, and our family was among them. My twin brother, Ron, came into the world ten minutes later. We had an older brother called Charles. My mum was called Violet and my dad was called Charles, though everybody called him Charlie, just like they do my older brother now.

I don't remember too much about Hoxton, except that my mum was very unhappy there. She wanted to move to Bethnal Green to be nearer her own mum and dad. Bethnal Green was only half a mile away from Hoxton but it was regarded as a better-class place to live. I don't know why, because there were as many people dying from malnutrition in Bethnal Green as in Hoxton.

When Ron and I were about six we moved to a house in Vallance Road, just off the Bethnal Green Road, which is a main road through Bethnal Green. It was number 178. It wasn't a palace. In fact, let's not mince words, it was a dump. It was the second house in a terrace of four, there was no bathroom and the lavatory was in the tiny back yard.

All day and all night trains would go roaring past the end of our yard, on their way in and out of Liverpool Street Station, one of the busiest stations in London. The noise was unbelievable. The housing was poor, the people were poor, although the area was full of pubs and the pubs always seemed to be busy. It was not a pretty place to live. There were a lot of viaducts, covered in soot, near where we lived. There were no green fields, of course, not even any grass to speak of. Even the trees looked bare and worn out.

We moved there just before the Second World War, and when war broke out it was a dangerous place to live because the Germans dropped so many bombs on that part of London. By the time the war was over, the Germans had destroyed 10,000 homes in Bethnal Green alone. Where we used to live was known as Deserters' Corner, because so many of the men who lived around there had deserted from the army or had ignored their call-up papers. The police and the army were always coming round looking for them, but the streets were like rabbit warrens and they didn't often catch anyone. In any case, they would only come looking for deserters in the daytime

3

because it was too dangerous for them to be on the streets of Bethnal Green at night. I tell you, it was a tough area. There was a lot of drinking and a lot of fighting.

I'll never forget the funerals. More would be spent on a man's funeral than he could ever have earned in a year alive. We were bloody poor and times were really hard, and yet I've got happy memories of my childhood.

We were wicked little bastards, really, always getting into scraps with other kids and sometimes with each other. Right from early on, when we were just nippers, we had a gang in our street and we used to have brick battles with kids from other streets. We loved to fight, Ron and I. Maybe it was because we came from a family of fighters, maybe because we were brought up in an area full of fighting men. I don't know. But a lot of people, over the years, have asked me what motivated Ron and me, what drove us on. Well, a lot of it was that we loved to fight, not necessarily to hurt other blokes, but just to fight. Even in later years, when money and power became our motivation, it was still a good scrap that we enjoyed most.

Maybe it is something to do with our surname, Kray. That K on the front makes it sound aggressive – much more than if we'd been called Gray. Maybe it's also something to do with the fact that we are identical twins. We were always telepathic, right from when we were toddlers. If one of us was happy or crying or wanted to go to the toilet, the other would be the same. If one of us was hurt, the other would start to cry, even if he was in another room. We could somehow communicate feelings to each other without even talking – we still can. Twins are special, particularly identical twins. Only three or four births in every thousand produce them. I read somewhere that a German doctor had done a lot of research into twins and he had discovered that a lot of identical twins turned to crime. And if one twin did something, the other would automatically follow.

The big influence in Ron's and my life was our mother. We loved her very much. Every morning I used to listen from my bedroom window to my mother singing in the backyard at Vallance Road, while she did her washing and hung it out on the clothesline. She had a beautiful, sweet voice and I used to enjoy listening to her sing 'Somewhere over the Rainbow' and 'White Cliffs of Dover'.

4

She was the kindest woman in the world. She never hit us – not even when we'd been right little bastards. And whenever any of the neighbours or the mother of some kid we'd bashed up complained about us, she'd always say, 'What, my twins? Never!' The thing was, she meant it. She thought the sun shone out of Ron and me.

Although I believe I was really destined to be a boxer – I know I was good enough to be a pro – someone or something – and maybe it was me – changed my destiny. I became a gangster, a villain, instead, and, by Christ, I've paid a hell of a price for it.

We came from a family of fighters. My grandad on my mum's side was a marvellous character. His name was John Lee, but they called him the Southpaw Cannonball because he could hit so hard, particularly with his left hand. Even when he was an old man he loved to punch an old mattress slung over the clothesline in the back yard. He used to sit Ron and me on his knee and tell us stories of the East End and its great fighters.

It was Grandad Lee who gave me my love of boxing. After listening to his stories, I would sometimes wake in the early hours of the morning. My bedroom overlooked the railway yard and I used to listen to the different sounds that came from the yard. They were like music in my ears. The sounds of horns in the distance, the guards' whistles, and the shunting of trucks. I would lie in my bed and imagine that one day I would follow in the footsteps of the great Jack Dempsey, who was known as the Manassa Mauler. He was the former heavyweight champion of the world, and at the start of his career as a fighter he was a hobo.

My dad, in those days, was nearly always on the run, usually from the army but also occasionally from the police. He was a small, dapper little bloke who, before the war, had been a pesterer – he'd travel round the better-class areas trying to persuade people to sell him their nick-nacks, bits of gold and silver, even clothing, which he would then resell for a profit. He was very good at it. He wasn't a fighting man, like the rest of the men in the family, but he was a hell of a drinker.

When the war began dad was ordered to report to the Tower of London, but he didn't fancy being in the army, so he did a bunk. He changed his name and for the next twelve years he was on the trot. They caught him once, but even then he managed to escape from

Woolwich Barracks in north London. During his years on the run it was difficult for him to make a proper living so he would occasionally have to resort to a bit of thieving and the like. The police tried to nail him a few times but he was too wily for them.

My dad being away meant a hell of a lot of responsibility for our mother, but she did brilliantly. She kept the family together, she kept us clothed and fed, though how she did it I'll never know. When our dad was away we were happy with our mum, but when he occasionally came back we were quite a happy little family. My dad had a lot of good ways. He would always polish our shoes and his own at night-time. And he always used to make sure the house was bolted, front and back, every night, although only a real prat would have tried to break into 178 Vallance Road.

When we were little kids we used to sell bundles of firewood around the streets of the East End to bring a bit more money into the house. Sometimes, when we were really skint, my mother would go to a pawn shop in the Bethnal Green Road and pawn what little bits of jewellery she had, tiny bits of gold or silver which she was saving for a rainy day, and Ron, Charlie and I would be really happy because we could buy something to eat. We would say to our mum, 'Well done, Mum.' And she would give us her lovely, warm smile. I'll never forget her smile.

During the war, when the air-raid siren would sound, our poor mother would grab our hands and drag us off to the air-raid shelter. She was terrified, not for herself, but in case any of us got hurt. I'll always remember the glare of the huge searchlights roaming the skies looking for German planes. They were just like huge torches. And the shrapnel falling from the sky, splattering the building walls. And the crying. And the hunger. And hiding in the railway arches near our home, and when the bombs stopped, the clatter of the train wheels in motion. And the dozens of other families who used to cower in those arches as well.

My grandfather, John Lee, would put on a little variety show in the arches just to amuse us all. Part of his act was to lick a white-hot poker. He explained to me that if the poker had been red-hot instead of white-hot, it would have burned his tongue off. He could also balance on top of a pile of bottles which were placed in tiers to form a sort of wall. He was incredible. Characters like him don't exist any more. Rough characters, yes, tough characters, yes, but real men.

We were eleven when the war ended and we started going to Daniel Street School, which is now called Daneford School, just a few streets from our home. One morning at school I got into a fight with a boy bigger and older than me. He blacked my eye and I knew then that, even if I was a good scrapper, I still didn't know enough about the techniques of boxing. I told my older brother Charlie, who by then was in the navy and starting to win a few navy boxing titles, and he said he would teach me to box properly. Ron said he'd like to learn as well. Mum let us have one of the bedrooms as a sparring room and Charlie got a navy kitbag which we stuffed and used as a punchbag, suspended from the ceiling. We used a meat hook to attach it to the floor.

Charlie was great. He would spar with us for hours at a time and teach us many boxing tricks and techniques. All the local kids used to come to our home-made gym and some of them later turned professional, like the Gill brothers, the Nicholsons and Charlie Page. We had some great times – perhaps the best times of our whole lives.

One time I was sparring with a boy and he caught his head on the concrete fireplace and knocked himself out. Another time, Ron Gill was afraid to hit a Sikh kid called Zoobla in case he knocked his turban off.

But then came the first time Ron and I ever stepped into a real boxing ring. There was a fair at a local park and it had an attraction called Stewart's Boxing Booth. There were some really tough fighters on the stand with names like Buster Osbourne, Steve Osbourne and Les Haycox. If a bloke could manage to stay in the ring for a few minutes with one of these characters he could earn a few bob. Usually, though, all most people got was a bloody nose.

This particular night no one was keen to go up and fight any of these guys. So the bloke on the stand says, 'Right, come on, isn't anyone going to fight?' Ron pipes up and says, 'Yes, I will.' Well, they all laughed at him, this little kid, and the bloke said, 'I think you're a bit too small, sonny.' So I shouted up that I would fight Ron. So we got in the booth and boxed each other. We had a hell of a scrap

7

and were paid 2s 6d between us. My dad thought it was funny when he heard the story, but our mother was very upset and made us promise never to do anything like it again.

Another good laugh came when my dad came home dead drunk one night. He crept through a window and went into the room we had converted into a gym. Unfortunately for him, he put his foot on the meat hook which was holding our punchball down. It went right through his foot and he was stuck there, cursing and swearing, until the doctor came to rescue him. We all had a bloody good laugh at him.

In the winter of 1948 I won the London Schoolboys Boxing Championship at the West Ham public baths. I was fifteen and I had qualified to box for the title after a series of fights in the divisional championships. My father came with me on the journey by bus to West Ham from Bethnal Green.

My first fight of the night was against a boy by the name of Patterson and I won comfortably on points. I rested in the dressing room before the final bout, which was for the championship itself. My opponent was called Roy Winterford. He was from West Ham, so he had the audience on his side. He got a tremendous roar when his name was announced. I could see he wasn't a novice – he had badges on his shorts which indicated that he was an area champion. But when the bell went I felt calm and confident. He was awkward to fight because he was a southpaw, but by the end of the first round I was ahead on points.

Then, in the second round, he caught me with a left hook to the solar plexus. It doesn't matter how strong your stomach muscles are, a punch to this area will double you up. But I was determined not to show Roy Winterford I was hurt. So I bent my head forward and started to bob and weave to conceal the fact that I was doubled over in agony. The ploy worked and Winterford missed his opportunity, because I coasted through the round. I won on points and the referee declared me 'Champion of London'.

I was very proud, and so was my dad. 'I wondered why you were bobbing and weaving with your head so much,' he said afterwards. 'I'd no idea he'd got you in the stomach.'

On the way home on the bus all the streets were lit up by the street lights, and, as I looked out of the bus window, I said to myself, 'I am champion of all those streets.' It was a great feeling. When I got home and told my mum, she was very proud.

I still have the badge that I got for winning the championship, which was to be worn on my shorts. Yes, that was a day I'll always remember.

So, you see, my life as a kid had its darker moments, but it also had moments of great happiness. There wasn't a lot of trouble with the law, no more than in the life of any other East End kid at the time. Sure, Ron and I liked to have a scrap, but all the kids who lived in that area at that time liked to fight. I had a few clips round the ear from coppers, but nothing more serious than that.

I get bloody upset when I read articles and books which say Ron and I had some curse over us when we were kids, that we were like children of the Devil, that we were evil. We weren't, we were just normal lads. Kids in the East End are probably not all that different now.

Occasionally I thought about the incident with the bread van, but the only real trouble I actually got into with the law was when I was about twelve. I got done for firing a slug gun – a sort of air pistol – out of the window of a train. We were on our way back to London after a day out picnicking at Chingford in Essex. We were just mucking about in the compartment of the train and I opened the window and fired a few pellets out. The guard grabbed hold of me and locked me in his cabin. I was 'under arrest' for the first time.

The police treated me like a hardened criminal. That was when I first really began to hate coppers. They went completely over the top and really upset my mum. It wasn't as if I'd hit anyone or hurt anyone, but still they took me to court. I was lucky. I got off with a warning.

The Reverend Hetherington, who ran a youth club near our home, spoke up for me in court – just as he did four years later, when I was sixteen and Ron and I got done for GBH (grievous bodily harm). The charge sheet stated that we caused GBH to Dennis Seigenberg, Walter Birch and Roy Harvey. The charges were read out in a small room at Hackney police station. There had been teenage gang warfare outside a dance hall in Mare Street in Hackney. Bike chains and coshes had been used by the rival gangs. It was a case of six of one, half a dozen of the other. Yes, we were involved, but so were they. But it was the Krays who were in bother, along with a couple of other lads, Tommy Organ from Bethnal Green and Pat Aucott, who came from Islington.

A few months later they had us up at the Old Bailey. Dear Reverend Hetherington spoke up on our behalf and we were acquitted of the charges. In his book *Profession of Violence* John Pearson seems to be saying that Ron and I and the others actually waited for Harvey in an alleyway and then set about him. That isn't true. Waiting in alleyways wasn't our style – we were totally up front with our fighting. Nobody scared us. Neither is it true that we tried to intimidate a girl witness by threatening to razor her if she spoke against us. The Kray twins did many bad things over the years but hurting women and children was never our style.

One of those involved in that punch-up was a lad called Dennis Seigenberg. Many years later, in 1969, I met him again in the special security block in Parkhurst prison. We were both at the start of life sentences. He hadn't changed a lot since I'd last seen him, but his name had. He was now calling himself Dennis Stafford and he'd been convicted of killing a fruit-machine salesman.

That appearance at the Old Bailey was the start of a long war between Reg and Ron Kray and the law. It was a war they eventually won – though we won quite a few battles along the way.

It was also the beginning of the end of what could have been a good boxing career. When I was sixteen I had seven fights as a professional and won them all. There wasn't the big money in boxing then like there is now, but I was good and I could have done all right. But managers and promoters don't like boxers who get into trouble with the law. Suddenly, in boxing circles, the name Kray had become bad news. So I just thought: Sod 'em. If I can't make a living one way, I'll make it another. I'd had too many years hungry. So had Ron. We had no intention of being hungry any more.

Ron: Born to Hang

In the East End, when we were kids, you really had only one of two choices if you wanted to make anything of yourself in life: you either became a boxer or a villain.

You always got the odd exception to the rule, of course. One of the kids who used to come to our house in Vallance Road was called Kenny Lynch, and he went on to become a good entertainer. He even got an MBE, which is pretty unusual for an East End backstreet urchin. Good luck to him, he was a great little fella. But we weren't properly educated, so there weren't that many options if we wanted to make a bob or two.

Our heroes were always boxers or villains. Our biggest hero was Ted 'Kid' Lewis, who was champion of the world at three separate weights. He grew up just round the corner from us and we worshipped him.

But we also really admired the famous local villains, like Jimmy Spinks, Timmy Hayes and the greatest of them all, Dodger Mullins and Wassle Newman. All great fighters, but in a different way to Ted. They were East End villains of the old style. Fearsome, tough fighting men who didn't give a toss for anyone. Even the coppers were scared stiff of them. They ruled the streets of the East End when we were kids, but they always played by rules which we admired. They never hurt women or kids or old people – they only ever did damage to their own kind. That was the code by which Reggie and I lived and we still believe it was right, even though we paid a high price for it.

Wassle Newman was the biggest man I ever saw, a giant of a man, with a beautiful set of white teeth, which he used to keep in good condition by chewing huge crusts of bread. One night he stopped at a tea and coffee stall in the East End – one of those wooden stalls – and he asked for a cup of tea and a crust. Well, they didn't have any crusts and that annoyed Wassle. So he got a length of chain and tied one end to the stall and the other end to a tram that was parked nearby. When the tram moved off, so did the stall. The whole lot moved a few yards, there was a bloody great bang – and then the stall collapsed in a heap. And the guy who ran the stall was still inside it. He was well pleased, I can tell you. But he took one look at Wassle and decided not to make an issue out of it. He was wise. You can always buy a new stall – it's more difficult to get a new face.

Dodger Mullins, though, was the real guv'nor of the East End in those days. My dad used to say he ran the area and most of the thieving that went on at that time. Most people steered well clear of

11

Dodger, but he was always kind to me and Reg and the other kids in the area.

Another hero was a tough guy called Harry Hopwood. He used to be at Vallance Road a lot when we were kids and he had been the best man at our parents' wedding. He used to sit us on his knee and get us to drink from bottles of brown and light ale. Years later he gave false evidence against us in court to save his own skin. Later I heard he'd died an alcoholic, which I thought was poetic justice. I wonder if, in his later years, when he knew he was dying, he ever thought about those little twins he used to bounce up and down on his knee.

So you see, when we were young, we were brought up against a background of fighting – a background of violence, if you like. There were always plenty of fights in the pubs and regular battles between the villains of Bethnal Green and the villains from other areas, like Watney Street in Whitechapel. The police rarely intervened in these scraps for the simple reason that they didn't want to get hurt themselves.

Our own family produced a lot of fighting men. They used to call my father's father Mad Jimmy Kray, because of his fierce temper and fighting ways. He had a clothes stall in Brick Lane market, and Reg and I sometimes used to help him load and unload his stuff. We've still got the medals he won for bravery in the First World War. He was a very brave man. They all were – fierce, aggressive, nasty maybe, but very brave.

My great grandfather's name was Critcha Lee. He was a gypsy, a cattle dealer from Bermondsey. He died in Claybury madhouse, and so did my grandfather's brother, whom they called Jewy. It seems that gypsy blood and madness have always run through the family.

Reg has spoken about John Lee, my grandad on my mum's side, the man they used to called the Southpaw Cannonball. He wasn't just a great fighting man, he was also a showman, an acrobat and juggler. He lived till he was ninety-eight and he was probably the most amazing man I've ever met. I even wrote a poem about him which I dedicated to the memory of grandad. It was called 'He Was a Man'.

First and foremost he was a man.
He had seen the gaslight era,

12

The Blitz,
And caught a glimpse of the permissive society.
Had done most things in his life.
Fought in the ring,
Danced on stage and would sing,
Leapt from barrels
And through rings.
Was around when Bob Fitzsimmons beat the great John I.,
Worked hard and fought well.
Could play most musical instruments,
Even licked a white-hot poker for fun,
Liked all sports
And would jump and run,
And always had a great story to tell.
Yes, he was a man.
He never knew the word of fear,
We loved him dear.
His precious memory we will keep.
He went to sleep in his ninety-eighth year,
God bless him and may he rest in peace.

Not the best of my poems maybe, but it sums up the kind of man he was, the kind of man you just don't find any more.

I admired all these men, but the two people I really loved were both women – my mother and my Auntie Rose.

My mother was simply a wonderful woman. No man ever had a finer mother. We often had no money and very little food, but she always made sure that Reggie and Charlie and I had something to eat and something half decent to wear. She always seemed to be cooking, washing or mending for us. She never gave in to despair or frustration, even when times were bleak and the future seemed to hold nothing. Even now, as I sit here in Broadmoor, wondering how it all went so wrong, I can still remember my mother holding me in her arms when I was little. I can still remember the smell of her soap. She was always spotless, even in all the grime and filth of the East End. She was the most placid woman I ever met. I never had an argument with her, we never answered her back, and I've never had a bad word to say about her. I would kill any man who spoke ill of my mother.

13

She loved making people happy. She used to tell me that God pays debts without money. She was always thanking God when something good happened.

And she was scrupulously fair. Sometimes Reg and I used to compete for her attention, to get in her good books the way kids do, but she would have none of it. We were always equal in her eyes. As well as a great closeness between Reg and me, there was always a bit of rivalry. One twin never wanted to be outdone by the other. Maybe that philosophy has added to our problems over the years, perhaps we've done unnecessary things just to prove to the other that we weren't chicken.

I also loved my mum's sister, my Auntie Rose, who lived round the corner from us in Vallance Road. She always had a soft spot for me; I think I was always her favourite from the time when I caught diptheria when I was very tiny and nearly died. She was a much harder woman than our mother, much tougher, and she wasn't frightened of any man, but she was always gentle with me. One day the kids at school had been taking the mickey out of me because my eyebrows were different from theirs – they went right across my nose and joined in the middle. I was upset about this and I asked my Auntie Rose why my eyebrows were like that. I'll always remember what she said: 'It means you were born to hang, Ronnie love.' As it happened, she was very nearly right. Perhaps it would have been better for me if her prediction had come true.

I don't have quite such happy memories as Reg about our father. During the periods he was at home he would often drink too much and come home and start shouting. This used to upset me and I used to think that one day, when I was bigger, I would give him a bloody good hiding – and later I did. Even as we grew up, when Reg and I started boxing and were training really hard, he would still come home drunk late at night and wake us with his shouting. He wasn't a bad man. But when he'd had a drink he got a bit silly. Looking back, though, times were so hard then that it's not surprising that blokes took to drink.

When war was declared and my father went on the trot from the army we were only six, but on the occasions when he did come round to Vallance Road he told us that if the police came looking for him we were to tell them that he had left home, that he wasn't living with our

14

mother any more. And he used to send us round the corner to the tobacconist to buy a newspaper, just to see if there were any coppers hanging around.

At that time he was living in a room in a house in south London with an old pickpocket called Bob Rolphe. Reggie, Mum and I would go over and see him in his room in Camberwell.

On two occasions he was actually at home at Vallance Road when the police called. One time he hid beneath the kitchen table, hidden by the tablecloth, while Reg and I were having our tea. He stayed there while a copper questioned us about our dad. We were both frightened but we gave nothing away. That was the first – and last – time a copper ever frightened me. Another time he was hiding in a cupboard and as a policeman was going to open the door I shouted out, 'You don't think my dad would hide in there, do you?' The copper shrugged his shoulders and went to look somewhere else.

Our mother tried to bring us up properly, but with a background like that it was impossible for us to have any respect for the law. It was always a case of them or us. Times were dreadful really, but I found the war ever so exciting. I loved the sound of the bombs and all the noise.

Shortly after war was declared in 1939 we were evacuated with our mum to a farm at Hadleigh in Suffolk. Reggie and I loved it there – we ran wild in the countryside. To this day we both love the smell and the feel of the countryside. But our mum missed the East End and all her family, so back we came to the East End.

I can still remember vividly the sound of the sirens going and Reggie, Mum and me going into a pitch-black street. I can remember seeing the searchlights in the sky and hearing the bombers overhead. I can remember the bombs dropping and us running to the air-raid shelter, an old railway arch, where we used to take cover. Everybody else was frightened, but I loved the excitement of it all.

I've always loved a good scrap, no matter who was involved. My mother used to tell us to say our prayers that the war would end, but I can remember praying that Adolf Hitler would get smashed by a bus. I told my mum, but she said it was wrong to pray for things like that, even though Hitler was a bad man. That sort of comment was typical of my mum.

I can remember, in Cheshire Street, just a street away from ours, one of Mosley's Blackshirts slagging off the Jews, and my grandfather arguing with him. God, the drama of it all, the colour, the sheer fucking excitement. I loved it. We kids used to play on the bomb sites and the dumps, staging our own wars. We caught scabies more than once and the medical officer came and painted us. We had great battles with kids from other streets, chucking all sorts of things at each other.

But it had to end and, when the war was over, we started proper schooling at Daniel Street. We also joined a small youth club in the Bethnal Green Road, run by the Reverend Hetherington, the man who helped Reggie when he got into trouble over the slug gun in the train. He was over six feet tall and very powerfully built. We never went to his church but we really liked him and often did odd jobs for him. We were a tough, unruly bunch of East End kids, but the Reverend Hetherington really knew how to handle us.

Funnily enough, we were happy at school too. It was never quite exciting enough for Reg and me, but the kids were encouraged to box and play football. We had a great football team. An East End newspaper has recently printed some pictures of the Daniel Street team of the time and called us 'the Liverpool of the thirties and forties'. The article says: 'The boys of Daniel Street, for many years, won everything – except the wooden spoon.'

There were pictures, too, of some of our old teachers – Mr Bell, Mr Faulkner and Mr Evans. They were good blokes and they knew how to handle us, old Bill Evans in particular. He was a teacher at Daniel Street for thirty years. He was a Welshman and we took the piss out of him for that. But he didn't mind, and if we went too far we got a good belt round the head. But it worked. There was a bloody sight more discipline then than there is in schools now. In one article Bill Evans was quoted as saying: 'The Kray twins were the salt of the earth. Never the slightest bother as long as you knew how to handle them. They were all right.'

Mind you, even old Bill Evans never sussed one of our tricks, and that was, if one of us was in trouble, he'd pretend to be the other one. We always used to confuse teachers like that. If a teacher would scream, 'I want a word with you, Reg,' then Reg would look up

16

innocently and say, 'But I'm Ron. I'm sorry but I don't know where Reg is!' By the time the teacher had eventually found the one he was after, he'd generally cooled down. It was a trick we pulled many times in later life – both with the army and the law.

Of course, there were fights at school. Reggie and I were evil little bastards when it came to a scrap and we would always make sure that the other kids came off worse. But we had to – even at school it was a survival of the toughest. But, as Reg says, we were never the children of the Devil that some people have painted us.

I don't know how many of our old teachers are still alive, if any, but as I write Father Hetherington is still alive, although he's now a very old man. But if he reads this, I would like him to know that we still think a lot of him and we hope that he still has some fond memories of us.

Actually, Reg's slug gun incident apart, there was no more trouble with the law until we were sixteen. Sure, there were one or two warnings about fighting, but all the kids then used to get into scraps. What else would you expect? We came from a rough environment, we never had the benefit of a good education or facilities like sports halls and all the other things that kids today get. Don't get me wrong, I don't resent today's kids and all the advantages they've got, but we were lucky to have food and clothes and a roof over our heads.

As I said earlier, if you came from our part of the world you were either going to be a boxer or a villain – and it looked as though all three of us, Reggie, Charlie and me, were all going to be good boxers. My older brother Charlie was welterweight champion of the Royal Navy. When he came out of the navy he boxed as a professional. He had twenty-five fights and lost only four of them.

The trouble with Charlie – and this is funny when you remember we are talking about a member of the Kray family – the trouble with Charlie is that he was too easy-going. He just didn't have enough of the killer instinct that champion fighters need. That's not a personal criticism – either you've got it or you ain't. Charlie was, and still is, a lovely, mild-mannered sort of bloke. I've only ever seen him lose his temper once – and that was the night he knocked out Jimmy Cornell, George Cornell's brother, in a club we owned called the Double R. Later I knocked out George Cornell himself – but rather more permanently. Those Cornells had a knack of looking for, and finding, big trouble.

When it came to boxing I was just the opposite of Charlie. I was a bit too aggressive, a bit too keen to get 'em flat on their backs and get the fight over with. But I didn't do too badly. I didn't get beaten much as an amateur and when I turned pro I won four fights out of six. I was a welterweight in those days.

But Reggie was the real star. London Schools Champion, virtually unbeaten as an amateur and, when he turned pro, he won seven out of seven as a lightweight. Reggie could have gone all the way, and I think in some ways it was my fault that he didn't. If one of us was going to get into real trouble with the law, it was always going to be me. There was something about my nature: if someone did something or said something which I didn't think was right, I'd slug 'em and that would be that. I loved my family and my friends, but I couldn't give a toss for other people. And I hated coppers ever since I was a nipper and they used to come round to our house looking for our dad. With an attitude like that, chances are you're going to get into bother sooner or later.

Reggie was different. He didn't always think like that. He liked a more peaceful life. But he was my twin, my other half. We looked the same, we thought the same. If I had a problem, he had a problem and vice versa. If I had a pain, he had a pain. And if I had an enemy, he had an enemy. So when I started getting into bother with the law, Reg was bound to follow me. He had to, he had no choice. It was like the law of nature. I hope I'm making myself clear, but maybe you've got to be one half of identical twins to know what I'm saying.

In those early days after we left school – and we left at fifteen – there wasn't any real bother. Just one or two small local punch-ups, and that was it. All we cared about was our boxing. We went to bed early every night, got up early every morning, no smoking or drinking, lots of running and training. We loved it. They were the best times.

We were getting more and more publicity in the London papers and I've kept every single clipping. There's one about when we fought at Lime Grove baths in a charity boxing night for a popular East End boxer called Wally Davis. The headline says: 'The Kray Twins Score Another Smart Double'.

The Kray brothers of Bethnal Green once again scored a winning double.

Reg outpointed Bill Sliney, of Kings Cross, over six rounds.

Ron ko'd George Goodsell, of Cambridge, in the fifth of their six-round contest.

So remorseless was Ron Kray that he sent Goodsell to the canvas no less than five times – the fifth time for keeps.

Another article from an East End newspaper says that we could go on and become as famous as another pair of sporting twins, the cricketers Alec and Eric Bedser. The same article describes our occupation as 'wardrobe dealers', although I can't ever remember dealing in wardrobes.

I like to sit and read through these old clippings and I've got about seven scrapbooks filled with them. Not just boxing clippings but also the less favourable newspaper headlines we made later on as we began our climb to the top of London's underworld.

Those headlines really began when we were sixteen and got arrested after the fight outside Barry's Dance Hall in Hackney – the fight which Reg has mentioned – in which the lad Harvey got a bit of a thrashing. It was well deserved, but he did what very few people in the East End did in those days: he broke the unofficial wall of silence and ratted on us to the law. Unforgivable.

Reg and I went up to the Old Bailey on a GBH charge, but the judge – Judge McClure – dismissed the case through lack of evidence. But before we left the dock he said to us, 'Don't go around thinking you are the Sabini brothers.' The Sabini brothers had been the bosses in London for some years previously. Years later our relations with them are close and Johnny Sabini, though now an older man, comes to see me in Broadmoor. Years later, of course, Reg and I were the bosses of London, and we were far bigger than the Sabinis had ever been.

2

Crime and Punishment

Ron: 1950–53

I hate uniforms. I've always hated them. I hate them for what they stand for. And I hate the people who wear them. Without their uniforms they're usually nothing. Nobodies.

I had my first real problem with a man with a uniform in the summer of 1950. I was seventeen at the time, and after that I seemed to have nothing but problems with little men who suddenly felt big when they'd got their uniform on. I was standing with Reg and a few of my other mates outside a café in the Bethnal Green Road on a Saturday afternoon. We weren't causing any bother, just standing around, having a chat and eyeing up the girls. Although, to be honest, even in those days I thought girls were a waste of bloody time. You could always have more of a laugh with the lads than you could with any girl.

Anyway, we're standing there, when suddenly – wallop. I feel this bloody great shove in my back which almost sends me arse over tit. I turned round and there's this young copper.

'Come on, now, move along,' he says. 'You're obstructing this pavement.'

I couldn't help myself. I smacked him straight in the gob. He didn't know where he was, not till he woke up, flat on his back, on the pavement. We all scarpered a bit sharpish.

I knew I wouldn't get away with it and, sure enough, just a few minutes later a squad car pulled up alongside us, two coppers jumped out, slapped me around a bit and slung me in the back of their car.

It all happened so quick Reggie could do nothing about it. He didn't have time to get involved. But he knew, as well as I did, that if you smacked a copper in the mouth and you got caught, well God help you when the other coppers got you back to the nick. They'd beat the f— out of you. And that's exactly what happened to me.

Dear old Reggie couldn't exactly come in and attack the whole police station single-handed, he does the next best thing. He walks back down the Bethnal Green Road, finds the young copper who pushed me in the first place, taps him on the shoulder, and when he turns round he smacks him straight in the gob. That's twins for you. Double trouble!

And we were in trouble, all right. Up in front of the magistrates I pleaded provocation, Reg said he'd only acted in my defence – which, in a way, he had – and dear Father Hetherington spoke on our behalf. We were lucky – we got probation. But, of course, it was just a few more bad headlines in the East End press to go with the good ones we were getting for our boxing. Even so, at that stage we weren't villains, just a couple of tough lads who could handle themselves if anyone got stroppy.

We might still have stayed on the straight and narrow, but a few months later, in the spring of 1952 – March, I'm sure it was – something happened that changed the whole course of life for Reg and me. *The army*. We were called up to the Tower of London to join the Royal Fusiliers for national service. We had a good chat about it and we decided that even though we were against the army on principle, and even though we hated the thought of wearing a bloody stupid uniform, we would give it a go as long as they would let us be PTIs (physical training instructors). After all, we were ideal men for the job, being young and fit. Not only that, but it would be very good for our boxing as well. We'd stay in good shape and probably get some good experience against the army champions. So, having made up our minds, we put on our best blue suits and went along to the Tower of London.

The first thing we came up against was a bird-brain in a bloody uniform, a corporal who thought he was Winston Churchill or Montgomery. We told him we wanted to be PTIs, otherwise we didn't want to be in the army, and he told us, 'Bloody well do what you're told.'

So we started to walk towards the door and he said, 'Where the bloody hell do you think you're going?' We said we were going home to Vallance Road. He said he didn't think that was a very good idea, and then he did a very silly thing – he held on to my arm and tried to stop me leaving.

I turned round and smacked him hard on the end of his jaw. Like the young copper, he was in dreamland for a few minutes. And Reg and I were on our way home to Vallance Road for a nice cup of tea with our mother.

That night we went to a dance hall in Tottenham and enjoyed ourselves. The next morning the army came and collected us from Vallance Road. There was no problem, no struggle. We knew we'd have to go back, we'd no intention of going on the run and being chased year after year. There's no fun in that. We still hoped the army would change its mind and let us be PTIs. But we weren't stupid and we both knew that this was just the start of what turned out to be two years of war between Ron and Reg Kray and the army.

When we got back to the Tower we were charged with being absent without leave and with striking an officer. The only trouble was they, like a lot of people before them, couldn't decide which one of us had actually thumped the corporal. And, of course, we didn't exactly help them.

'Was it you who struck the corporal, Reg Kray?' the CO asked.

'Oh, no sir,' said Reg.

'Then it must have been you who did it, Ron Kray?' said the CO.

'What, me sir? Oh, no sir.'

'Well, one of you did it.'

'No sir, not us sir'.

And so it went on. Round and round in circles – the old 'who's who?' trick we'd pulled before so many times at school.

But the CO wasn't stupid either. As he couldn't decide which one of us had done it, he gave us both seven days in the guardroom. We weren't happy about it, I can tell you, and we decided we were going to make the army pay for the way it was treating us.

Our dad came to visit us while we were in the guardroom. He was on the run himself at the time, so it was an extremely dangerous thing to do. But he disguised himself, pretending he was one of our uncles, and got away with it.

That was the only good thing about that week and we couldn't wait for it to end. Our plan was quite simple. The moment they released us from the guardroom, we were going to leg it. There was no way now that we were going to make it simple for them.

And that's exactly what we did. In the guardroom we'd made friends with a bloke called Dickie who was also in trouble. He was from the East End as well. The three of us decided to do a bunk together. We went to stay for a while at Dickie Hughs' home in Clinton Road, but the police soon came sniffing round there, so we had to move on. It was the same story at our own home. It was a tricky time and we relied heavily on others to help us.

But East Enders, in particular, do help each other in times of trouble, especially if it means getting one over on the dreaded law. We had some great friends at that time. There was a man called Jack, who used to work in a café in the East End. When Reg and I were on the run he'd kindly give us supper every night – chips, sausages and eggs, cups of tea, even cigarettes. We will never forget his kindness. Years later he went to our mother's funeral. He was a good man. So was another Jewish guy we knew as Yossel, who used to frequent a Lyons Corner House in the West End. He used to buy all the young guys who were on the run from the army a really hearty breakfast. I don't know why – maybe he just hated the army. But we were grateful for the man's kindness and grateful, also, that he used to take our mother flowers when we were in Parkhurst.

It was around this time that Reg and I started getting into bad habits. Until then we'd been really fit, really looked after ourselves. Now, though, we started to smoke and drink and keep what might be termed bad company. Don't ask me why, I guess it was inevitable. It may have been mainly my fault, I don't know, but it was certainly a case of twins wanting to be together and be alike.

We still loved a good punch-up and I can recall one tremendous scrap at the Royal Ballroom in Tottenham during the time we were on the run. It started the way those fights always did, with Reg, Dickie Hughs and me swaggering in like we owned the joint, knowing full well it was full of lads from Tottenham. Then we'd start to eye up the local crumpet, make a comment or two to them, knowing it would drive some of the local lads wild. One of them walked up to Reg and told him to 'Piss off.' Whack! The Tottenham lad was on the floor, minus four or five teeth, and suddenly it was like a saloon in the old Wild West – everybody slugging everybody else, chairs flying everywhere – it didn't matter who you hit as long as you kept hitting them – And Reg and me, side by side, smashing the bastards up. It was great. Meanwhile, on the stage, there's Lita Roza singing her heart out and Ray Ellington and his band trying to play on as if nothing was happening! Years later we became great friends of Lita Roza, though she never did share our fond memories for those epic nights at the Royal!

Was it stupid? Yes, of course it was. Were we yobbos? Yes, of course we were. I don't know why we did it. It seems silly now, and I feel sorry for any innocent bystanders caught up in our battles. If you were one of them, well, my apologies. I've quietened down a bit now.

During that particular spell on the run, which lasted a few weeks, we even 'borrowed' a car and went to Southend. We sent the commanding officer at the Tower a postcard from the seaside, saying something like 'Having a lovely time, wish you were here. Best of luck, Ron, Reg and Dick.' At least the CO had a sense of humour. When we got back to the Tower we found he'd stuck our card on the wall.

But our freedom couldn't last and, quite honestly, we didn't want it to. We didn't want to be like our dad, permanently on the run. We had to get this stupid army business out of the way, once and for all.

We were finally spotted in a café in the Mile End Road by a copper by the name of Fisher. We gave up without a struggle and it was back to the detention cells. Another dust-up with the officers and we were off to the detention barracks at Colchester for a month. Then it was back to the Tower and, just to show 'em, Reg and I decided to do another bunk. We stayed with various friends around London and even managed to do a bit of unofficial boxing.

I remember I boxed at an unlicensed show at Bexley in Kent. I was matched against a farmer and he started to butt me in the face. So I kneed him in the groin. The crowd wanted to lynch me, but I won the fight and collected a fiver. Apart from that we were always clean fighters and later we did a lot for kids' boxing clubs in the East End. We would take people like Rocky Marciano and George Raft along to meet the local kids.

It was during this particular spell on the run that Reg and I discovered our love of snooker and realized the possibilities of making money out of snooker halls. We also began making really useful contacts in the criminal underworld, contacts that were to stand us in good stead in later years.

Ironically, this particular spell of freedom was almost ended by the copper who caught us before – Fisher. But this time we weren't in such good humour. We were sitting in another café in the Mile End Road when up he came.

'Come on, you bloody deserters,' he said. Perhaps it was the way he said it, but I took umbrage and smacked him in the gob.

They caught us a few weeks later and this time did us for assaulting a police officer in the course of his duty. For that we got a month in Wormwood Scrubs. We also got some bad headlines in the East End newspapers, but we made more useful contacts in the Scrubs for our future careers as criminals.

After the Scrubs we were taken by an army escort to Canterbury barracks. They kept us waiting three months for a court martial, so we really played them up.

By now it was the spring of 1953 and I guess this was the time I started to go a bit mad. I wouldn't wash, I would only shave half my face, I would act the fool. I thought it was funny at the time and that I knew exactly what I was doing. Now, though, I'm not so sure. Three years later I was certified insane.

Eventually we escaped from Canterbury. It was quite easy to get out of the barracks because they left ladders lying around. They clearly thought no one was going to bother to escape.

We'd fixed up to have a mate waiting with a van outside the barracks and he was going to drive us to London and freedom. Unfortunately, just a few miles up the road, the van broke down. So we all started walking to London until along came some motorcycle police and an army truck, and we were on the way back. We didn't struggle, there was no point. They gave us nine months' imprisonment at Shepton Mallet. After that they gave up on the Kray twins and kicked us out of the British Army. We regarded it as a victory. While we were in Shepton Mallet we met Charlie Richardson, who was also doing nine months. We got along fine with him without realizing that our paths were going to cross so dramatically in the years to come.

Actually, because of another misdemeanor in Shepton Mallet, Reg was due out three days after me. It seemed a pity that we wouldn't be ending our careers in the army on the same day, so I asked the captain if I could stay for an extra three days. He said to me, 'If you do anything wrong I'll be forced to keep you.' So I got myself caught smoking a cigarette on duty and was given the extra three days. And so ended the distinguished military careers of Ronald and Reginald Kray.

Reg: 1951–55

By 1954 we were free men again. It was the year we were twenty-one. Not only did we have the key of the door to Vallance Road, so to speak, but we also had the key of the door to our very first business venture – a billiard hall called the Regal in Mile End.

Before we took over local thugs had been causing a lot of trouble: tables were being ripped, glasses broken, there were fights all the time and staff kept coming and going. Decent people were frightened to go in there. The guy running it even bought a vicious Alsatian dog which he kept behind the counter. But that didn't worry the local tearaways – they used to chuck fireworks over the counter and eventually drove the dog mad.

It has been claimed that Ron and I were the ringleaders behind all this trouble, deliberately trying to cause problems so that we could muscle in ourselves. This was not the case. There had been many problems at the Regal long before we came on the scene. Eventually the owner of the building got fed up and chucked out the Regal's manager. So Ron and I went to see the owner, who said he'd let us have the lease if we could guarantee to keep the place under control and undamaged. He said he'd give us a month's trial.

As soon as we took over the trouble stopped. It was very simple: the punters, the local tearaways, knew that if there was any trouble, if anything got broken, Ron and I would simply break their bones.

We eventually got the lease for three years. We borrowed some money, moved in fourteen tables, second-hand but in good nick, and redecorated the place. We worked hard and it was packed day and night. We were only paying five quid a week in rent and soon were making a lot of money.

It was then that we got our first experience of the so-called protection racket. A Maltese gang came in and demanded protection money. We went straight for them with knives and never saw them again. They've not got a lot of bottle, these continentals, especially when the knives come out.

I'd better explain how the protection racket works, because it was big business then and it's still big business now in almost all large cities. A gang would offer to protect clubs, pubs, shops and the like from other gangs, in return for a fee. Often, of course, the business concerned was not in any danger from other gangs, but if the owner or manager of the business was to make this point and refuse to pay the protection fee, he would generally find that his business had been burgled, set fire to or generally smashed up. By then, of course, he was more than ready to pay his fee. Very few business owners went to the law because, if they did, the matter became personal and they themselves would become the target of the gang.

The protection racket has always been rife, even before the days of organized crime. When we were kids the likes of Dodger Mullins and Wassle Newman used to operate simple protection rackets, only they tended to take food and drink in return for making sure a shopkeeper wasn't bothered by other toughs.

It's an odious form of crime really, although in some of the tougher areas, where a number of gangs operate, it's sometimes the only way of getting a bit of law and order. Otherwise businesses can finish up paying protection money to several different individuals at the same time.

But, as you can imagine, we were horrified when those Maltese boys tried to put the squeeze on us. We were just about the worst people they could have picked on.

We were fearless in those days. Fighting was our game. When we got bored we would team up with our mates from the billiard hall and go to a dance hall or pub, just looking for a bit of bother. We never got beaten. We were big drinkers but we never seemed to get drunk. Those were wild and wonderful days. At that stage we weren't really villains, more like Jack the lads, certainly no worse than Teddy Boys.

It was around that time that the Kray gang was formed. It wasn't something deliberate, it just happened. Blokes seemed to congregate

27

naturally around Ron and me. Local villains – thieves and the like – would come to us with goods they had stolen and ask us to hide stuff. We would charge them a percentage for this. Once or twice we hid weapons for people, and I think it was that that started Ron's interest in guns.

Then the protection racket reared its ugly head again. A gang from over Poplar way tried it on us, but we soon smashed them up and two of them were quite badly hurt. Suddenly we saw the possibilities that the protection business might hold for us. After all, with our friends we were the most feared people in our part of the East End. So we devised our own protection business and it was soon working well. It may sound silly, but I believe we *were* offering a real service. Things had got completely out of hand in the East End and we brought some law and order where previously two or three gangs a week had been calling for protection money.

With us there were two kinds of payment, you were either on the Nipping list or on the Pension list. The Nipping list was those places where we could pop in if we needed a quick crate of gin or scotch or a case or two of champagne: pubs, off-licences, small shops and the like. The publicans and shopkeepers were actually well pleased. We were providing them with total protection in what was a very rough area for next to nothing. The Pension list was for more up-market places: restaurants, gambling joints and so on. They paid more, but not a vast amount of money; they were on a fixed rate which depended on the sort of turnover we thought they were doing. We didn't charge the earth, but none the less we now had a tidy sum coming into the old coffers every week.

Mind you, we had to provide a service. Other gangs would occasionally try to muscle in and would call round at a business we were protecting. We'd have a couple of our boys waiting for them next time they called. They generally got the message. If they didn't they'd get a broken nose instead. OK, so it wasn't straight. But what is straight anyway? All these so-called businessmen using lawyers and accountants to fiddle their books to cheat the tax man and the VAT man? I reckon they are as guilty as we were. Occasionally we would have to resort to violence, but only when it was necessary, and only against members of other gangs.

We still lived the simple life at Vallance Road. Our mum still looked after us and we didn't even have a car. The only real luxury was having our hair cut at home by a local barber. We got that idea from an American gangster film.

By 1955 the Kray name was getting more well known around London, though London in those days was really run by two guys – Billy Hill and Jack Comer, who was known as Jack Spot. They were the undisputed kings of the underworld. They were into everything: night clubs, spielers (drinking clubs), gambling clubs and prostitution. Then they fell out and Jack Spot came to see us. He wanted Ron and me to act as his bodyguards because he feared an attack by Hill and felt he couldn't trust some of his own men. It wasn't really our kind of work and we didn't much like Spot, but it was a good in for us at a higher level than we'd been in previously. So we travelled around with Spot for a while and made sure he never got into any bother. Then he paid us off and, unluckily for him, got carved up a few weeks later outside his flat in Bayswater. That was enough for him and he decided to quit. So did Billy Hill, who went off to live in Spain.

They didn't leave behind any real successors, just a number of gangs which were operating in different parts of London. The time was ripe for someone to move in and take over. Ron and I really fancied our chances. By now our firm (gang) was growing and we had quite a few blokes on the payroll, even though we were still based in the East End. We'd got our protection business, we'd got several little spielers and gambling clubs. We were the big men in the East End. But the question was: could we make it into the West End where the really big money was? We decided there was only one way to find out.

Ron: 1955–59

1955 was a memorable year. Reg and I were beginning our move towards the West End – and I shot my first man. He was a docker, an ex-boxer, who was trying to put the frighteners on the owner of a garage we were protecting. The garage owner was scared out of his wits, but he had the good sense to tell him he was short of readies and asked him to come back the following night. Then, said the garage owner, he'd have the necessary cash. In the meantime, of course, he was straight on the phone to us.

I was bloody livid. After all, here was this guy paying us good money to keep unsavoury individuals away, and here was the ex-boxer, who knew the garage was on our patch, trying to muscle in. He had to be taught a lesson. So when he came back the next night I was there waiting for him with a Luger pistol.

I was feeling really excited that night. When the fool started giving me a bit of mouth and started to get a bit threatening I shot him in the leg. I was thinking to myself: that's the last time that stupid bastard will ever try it on with the Krays.

Reggie wasn't too pleased when he heard what had happened and there was a bit of heat from the police for a while. We visited the guy we shot in hospital and told him to keep his mouth shut, or else we'd really do a job on him when he came out. And, to show there were no hard feelings, we gave his wife a bit of money – a few grand in fact – just to tide her over and make sure she didn't start getting lippy to the law.

The police came round to Vallance Road and said they wanted me to attend an identification parade. We were a bit concerned that Shorty might be stupid and pick me out, so Reg went in my place. The idea was that if Shorty did pick Reg out, then Reg would say, 'You've got the wrong one, I'm *Reggie* Kray!' That way I would have been forewarned and could have gone on the run. As it happened, Shorty was sensible and didn't pick anyone out.

Reg and I had a few words once the incident was over, but the fact of the matter was that it didn't do my reputation any harm at all. On the contrary, it did it the world of good. There were plenty of hard men in London in those days, but not many who were prepared to use a shooter. The whole thing helped to make the Krays, and me in particular, something to be avoided at all costs.

No sooner was this little bit of bother sorted out, than Reggie and I got what we'd always wanted – a foothold in the West End. A guy called Billy Jones had taken over a West End drinking club called Stragglers just off Cambridge Circus. But it was being ruined by constant fights between various characters who thought they could demand a spot of protection and make a name for themselves. These fights were expensive: they caused damage, they drove away decent customers who wanted to drink in peace and, most serious of all, they upset the law, who were threatening to close the place down unless things got much quieter. So Billy Jones's partner, an old boxing mate of ours called Bobby Ramsey, called us in as informal partners. The deal was that we'd get a share of the takings in exchange for making sure the trouble stopped. Within no time, of course, Reggie and I had banged a few heads together, told one or two characters that they were no longer welcome, and there was no more trouble. Peace reigned, and the money started pouring in.

It was too good to last, though, and sure enough it didn't. Bobby Ramsey was attacked and beaten up by a gang of Irish dockers who called themselves the Watney Streeters. They were upset because a couple of them had been thrown out of Stragglers and they decided to take it out on Bobby.

We had to get our own back, of course; otherwise we'd have lost all the control we'd worked so hard to gain. We made a few inquiries and discovered that this gang were to be found early most nights in a pub called the Britannic. About a dozen of us were waiting for them one night. There was a tremendous battle and one of them, a geezer called Jackie Martin, got very badly hurt. Unfortunately he did an unforgivable thing – he broke the East End code of silence and named me as the man who'd hurt him. He also named Bobby Ramsey and Billy Jones.

It meant that Martin was finished in London, of course. He had to beat a very hasty retreat. But it also meant that Ramsey, Jones and I were charged at the Old Bailey with grievous bodily harm. I got three years, Ramsey got five years because of his previous record, and Jones got three years. So by November 1956 I was in Wandsworth. I was twenty-three, I was one of London's most feared gangsters, I had a record, and I had shot a man. For a poor East End boy I had already made a bit of a name for myself.

Wandsworth was no problem for me. I very soon became the biggest tobacco baron in the place. I was making money inside and our businesses outside were going from strength to strength. But then, two years later, with the end of my sentence in sight, my life started to go wrong. I began to go mad again.

31

It happened when they sent me to Camp Hill, a soft prison on the Isle of Wight, for the last few months of my sentence. It was such a doddle there, just like a holiday camp, yet I hated it. It seemed so far away from home and my friends and family and Reg. It was great for them up in the Smoke, but I wasn't a part of it. I got depressed and withdrawn. I didn't want to know anything or anybody.

Then I heard that my Auntie Rose had died of leukaemia. I went beserk.

That's when my paranoia started. I began feeling that people were plotting against me. If I saw two people chatting I was convinced they were planning how they were going to get me. So I just had to stop them, hurt them, make them see what they were doing was wrong. Without my drugs I still get the same feelings today. I was taken to the psychiatric wing of Winchester prison and declared insane.

I was sent to Long Grove mental hospital near Epsom. I was in an awful state. I thought the bloke in the opposite bed was a dog. I couldn't recognize anyone. I kept putting my hand through the glass in the windows. It was hell. But they put me on strong drugs and gradually I started to feel a bit better, though I knew I wasn't right.

The family were really worried about my condition. They were worried that the authorities were going to use this as an excuse to keep me locked away for the rest of my life. That's when Reg decided to swop places with me. He and Charlie reckoned that if I got out and managed to stay out without getting into trouble, it would show the authorities that I wasn't insane any more and they would have to release me from custody. And that, in fact, is more or less what happened.

The swop was so easy it was monstrous. Reg and Charlie came to see me, and as they stood by my bed Reg said in a loud voice, 'I must go to the toilet.' And off he went. A couple of minutes later I said to Charlie – again in a loud voice so anyone nearby could hear – 'I think I must go and have a pee as well.' Reg was waiting for me in the cubicle in the toilet. He took off his clothes and I took off my pyjamas and we did a swop. Then we walked back to my bed, only this time it was Reg who climbed in and, half an hour later, it was me who left the mental hospital with Charlie.

Reg gave us time to get clean away and then he calmly walked up to the officer on duty and said, 'I'm going home now.'

'But you can't,' said the officer.

'Oh yes I can. My name is Reggie Kray and if you don't believe it here's my driving licence.'

They had no choice but to let him go, even though the police came and grilled him. He just said he had felt tired and decided to lie down, and when he woke up I was gone. It sounds silly, I know, but it's amazing how easy it is to deceive the authorities, particularly if you've got the nerve – and a twin brother.

But though I can joke about it now, that was a bad time for me. I stayed free for a few months, spending most of my time living in a caravan on a farm in Suffolk, owned by a friend. Occasionally Charlie and Reg would take me up to London, but not often. Then I went back voluntarily to Long Grove. I got a rollicking, of course, but soon after that they said I was fit enough to finish my sentence, so I returned to Wandsworth, and they let me out in early 1959. For a while I was treated at the St Clement's mental hospital in the Mile End Road, but in the end I stopped going there. I still wasn't right: I kept getting these urges to kill people because I was convinced they were plotting to kill me.

Shortly after I got out of Wandsworth, I became very friendly with an Italian fellow by the name of Battles. He asked me to have a drink with him one night in a club called the Central in Clerkenwell, a popular meeting place for many of the Italians in London at that time. While we were there Battles had an argument with another fellow by the name of Billy Alco. It all got a bit heated, nothing more, and then Alco went across to sit with some of his mates. I saw them talking, their heads together, and looking over at Battles and me. That did it. I was convinced Alco and his mates were plotting against me.

I had a revolver on me at the time and I took it out and had a shot at Alco. Luckily I missed, but the shot caused fucking chaos in the club. I was ready to shoot them all, but Battles held my arm and said to me very quietly, 'It's not necessary, Ron, let's go.' Something in the way he said it brought me to my senses and we left. Just as well, really, otherwise I might have massacred half the Italians in London. But I tell this story because it shows that I really did have problems, even at that time.

The funny thing is, Billy Alco – the guy I tried to kill – later turned out to be one of the best friends I ever had. He comes to see me in Broadmoor and is a real gentleman. So often the people we've tried to hurt have turned out to be our best friends later on.

Reg: 1959–64

After Ron was put away for the attack on Jackie Martin it didn't take the law long to close down Stragglers. But it didn't really matter because Charlie and I were now working together more closely and we were successful in our other business ventures.

I never forgot about Ron, though. While he was inside I bought an empty shop in the Bow Road and turned it into a club. I called it the Double R – a sort of tribute to Ron. Above the club we built a very snazzy gym and I got Henry Cooper to open it.

The Double R did well. Queenie Watts, the cockney singer, came there a lot. So too did Barbara Windsor, Sybil Burton and many other famous names. I got on particularly well with Barbara Windsor and those days were the start of a friendship that's lasted right until now. She's a bloody wonderful person who's managed to ride out some very difficult times. My brother Charlie played a big part in making the Double R a success. We haven't always seen eye to eye, Charlie and I, and even these days we occasionally fall out, but he certainly played his part in one of the most successful Kray ventures ever. He was married at the time to a girl called Dolly who always thought she was above the lot of us, and they had a couple of kids.

I loved my life in the late fifties. I made a lot of money but I was a good club owner. I was always there, I ran my club properly, as well as keeping an eye on our other little interests. These included a drinking club at Stratford in the East End, a financial interest in several second-hand car businesses, plus, would you believe, an illegal gambling club right next door to Bow police station. It took ages for them to sus us, but most coppers are as dim as Toc H lamps. That's been my experience, and I've had more experience than most. But even though I was so busy I never forgot about Ron and often went to visit him at Wandsworth.

On one of those visits I met Frank Mitchell, later to be known as the Mad Axeman and soon to play such an important part in our lives. Ron and Frank got on very well and Ron told him we would look after him when they both got outside.

I also got involved with a small-time hood called Ronnie Marwood, and that involvement probably cost us a small fortune. The police were turning a relatively blind eye to our drinking and gambling clubs for the simple reason that they were well run and there was never any trouble. The police aren't altogether stupid; they know that there will always be drinking and gambling clubs, but it's much better if they are well run. That way they don't give the law too many problems. So the coppers were leaving me fairly well alone until one night this face called Ronnie Marwood comes to see me. He was in a right state. He told me he'd stabbed a copper and wanted me to hide him.

I owed Marwood nothing and I knew he was going to cause me nothing but trouble. But, despite what they say, there is some kind of honour among thieves, a sort of code of conduct. Right or wrong, I took Marwood in and hid him in a safe place until he was ready to make a run for it.

The police came to see me, and in so many words they said, 'Tell us where Marwood is and we'll give you a free rein on your clubs, turn a blind eye.' But I couldn't. I told the police, 'I'm sorry, you're on one side, I'm on the other. I can't tell you where Marwood is.'

After that it didn't take the law long to shut down the Double R – they can always find a problem with your licence – and after that every club and business we owned was persecuted by the police. And all because we tried to help someone out.

Not only were we having problems with the law over the next three years, we were also very worried about Ron. His mental state really went downhill after they moved him to Camp Hill on the Isle of Wight. Suddenly Reggie and Ronnie Kray, the golden boys, seemed to have lost a bit of their glitter. But gradually Ron got back to being more like his old self and we were making a very steady income

35

looking after the business interests which Billy Hill still controlled in London. These were mainly gambling clubs and Billy was pleased with the work we did for him. As a result he gave us some good advice. 'Go a bit up-market,' he said. 'Get yourself a really decent club, then the coppers have got no reason to give you a hard time.'

And that's exactly what we did. In the summer of 1962 we opened a club called the Kentucky in the Mile End Road in Stepney. It was really smart. We spent a fortune on it. Two thousand pounds alone on carpets, lighting and wall-to-ceiling mirrors. Two grand may not sound much today but in the early sixties it was a lot of bread, particularly for a couple of working-class lads from the East End.

Early in 1963, a few months after we'd opened the Kentucky, Barbara Windsor asked me if we would let the club be used for some scenes in the film *Sparrows Can't Sing*, which starred Barbara, James Booth and Queenie Watts, and was directed by Joan Littlewood. I agreed and we were paid a decent sum of money by the film company. At the end of the year the film's premiere was held at a cinema in Stepney and there were some big names present, including Lord Snowdon and Roger Moore. My family and friends all attended – in fact, we bought the majority of the tickets. Afterwards, most of the cast and dozens of other celebrities came back for a party at the Kentucky.

It was on that night, with Ron and me done up like dogs' dinners in our bow ties and dinner jackets, and surrounded by the rich and the famous, that I realized that we were well on the way to making it to the very top. I felt so powerful that night. I felt nothing was going to stop us. The good times were back for the Kray twins, and, by Christ, we did have some good times and some good laughs at the Kentucky.

By today's standards the Kentucky was probably a bit loud and garish. It was all deep red carpets, mirrors and sprayed-gold 'antique' chairs and furniture. But the Kentucky was right for the time and, more especially, right for the toffs who wanted to come over from the West End and see a bit of the seamy side of life without having to get themselves dirty or put themselves in any danger. They loved it. It was exciting, it was exhilarating. They could kid themselves it was dangerous because there were plenty of evil-looking gangsters around. But they were actually as safe as houses. We ran a very tight ship indeed. There were never any problems at our club.

But if these rich punters wanted to pay well over the top for their food and drink and then lose a good few bob on the gaming tables, that was all right by us. They wanted fantasy – and we provided it. We also provided some novel entertainment which the toffs could go home and tell their hoity-toity friends about.

One of the stage acts we used was called Tex the Dwarf. He was a midget who wore an enormous Texan hat. He would climb on the back of a donkey and strum away on a guitar and sing cowboy songs. At the end of the act Ron would walk to the stage and lead the donkey over to the bar by its reins.

One night Ron had just led the donkey over to the corner of the bar and he'd got the donkey's reins in his left hand and a large glass of gin and tonic in his right. At that moment in walked a bookmaker who owed Ron a large amount of money. When Ron spotted the bookmaker he went bloody beserk and started telling the bookie he better pay up or else.

I just stood watching – it was bloody hilarious: there was Ron, gesticulating and laying down the law in general, with a donkey in one hand and a gin and tonic in the other. The bookie didn't seem to see the funny side of it, though, and sped out of the club fairly promptly.

Ron could be a very funny man, often without trying, and yet this is a side of him that is never portrayed. A few years later he was on the run from the police for about a year. There was a warrant out for him. During this time he used many aliases and disguises and was living in a secret flat in west London. One day he wanted to visit a friend in Bow in the East End. As this was obviously an area where the law would be looking for him, Ron decided to cover his face in bandages covered in tomato sauce, to make it look like he'd had an accident. For some reason he thought that this was an ideal disguise and that no one would possibly recognize him. Just as he knocked on the door of the house in Bow, a bloke who was passing by said, 'Hello, Ron, how are you keeping?' Ron was as sick as a parrot!

Like I say, he could be a very funny man. He still is, often without realizing it. I went to see him in Broadmoor shortly after the publication of a book I helped write called *Slang*. It was all about East End rhyming slang and I told Ron I had sent a copy to Ronald Reagan, the President of the United States.

'Oh yeah,' said Ron, 'what did he think of it?'

The good times came to an end when the police closed the Kentucky down a year later in 1964. They objected to us having a licence and took their objections to Stepney Borough Council. We were very upset because we felt this was blatant persecution and they told a lot of lies about us, how we were running the club badly, illegal drinking and gaming, etc. Is it any wonder we turned more and more to our protection business to make money?

Peter Rachman, the London landlord who received a lot of publicity at the time of the Keeler–Profumo affair for his extortionate rents and bully-boy tactics, was paying us for protection. He had to – it was either that or his rent collectors were set upon. They were big, but our boys were bigger. He didn't want to pay up. He avoided us at first and then sent a cheque that bounced. Silly. After that it was his rent collectors who started bouncing, and the unpleasant Mr Rachman started to see the error of his ways.

We never minded putting the squeeze on characters like Rachman, who made his money out of the misery of others and out of prostitution. An odious sort of person, though you had to admire him in some ways. His background was even poorer than ours. He was a Pole who slipped into Britain in 1946, at the age of twenty-seven, with just sixty quid in his pocket. When he died of a heart attack in 1962 he was worth millions. Who says crime doesn't pay?

But Ron and I never really liked the protection business. It wasn't glamorous enough for us. We longed to get back into club life in a big way. So, despite all the problems we'd had, we opened up our first legitimate night club in the West End. And it bloody nearly broke us.

Ron: 1964–65

Esmerelda's Barn it was called, in Wilton Place, Knightsbridge, a real posh West End club – and it was ours. We were good club owners, we worked long hours as hosts to the many celebrities and the rich young bloods who came to the club. But it was essentially a gambling club, and maybe we didn't know enough about managing a gambling club at this sort of level. After about a year we pulled out. Fortunes were won at Esmerelda's Barn, and a fortune was lost – ours.

We made a lot of mistakes. We thought it was enough to have a real-life lord – Lord Effingham, in fact – on the board of directors and a staff who had experience. We were wrong. Lord Effingham was a nice enough bloke. He was a close personal friend and we shared some similar interests. But we were done for a fortune by the staff and also by many of our customers, the rich and the famous, people whose word we trusted, who ran up fantastic gambling debts and then couldn't, or wouldn't, pay them. Sure, we chased them. But with that kind of customer – the sons of lords and earls, and film stars and so so – you can't go around banging their heads together or they go screaming to daddy or to the press. There's a bloody sight more honour among thieves than there is among the so-called aristocracy. For the first time in our lives Reggie and I were done for a lot of bread, and there was bugger all we could do about it.

What did for us more than anything was the book work. We had an accountant who cooked the books, didn't pay any tax, and then scarpered. If he's reading this, he'll know who he is. Tell you what, Mr X, why not pop along to Broadmoor for a little chat? There's still a few things for you and me to discuss.

The dear old Inland Revenue moved in like barracuda. Funnily enough, most of America's top gangsters – and that includes Al Capone – have been nailed, not by the police, but by the Inland Revenue. They effectively put us out of business at Esmerelda's Barn and almost into the nick. It was a case of 'pay up or go inside', and for once we had no choice. We had to cough up. So, by the end of 1964, we were out of the West End in a big way, with our fingers just a bit burned.

We also lost a packet in 1963–64 in a building project in Enugu in Nigeria, which was later to become Biafra. It was Ernest Shinwell, the son of the Labour peer Manny Shinwell, who got Reggie and me interested in this one. By this stage of our careers we were worth a few hundred thousand pounds and we didn't know what to do with it. We were still a couple of East End boys with simple tastes. Sure, by now we had a flash motor and good clothes and we used to take expensive holidays to places like Tangiers with people like Billy Hill and his girlfriend Gypsy, but basically we had more than we could spend and were looking for ways to invest it, a sort of pension for when we got too old for villainy. We wanted something with a bit more security than clubs. So along came Ernest Shinwell with this project he'd become involved in in eastern Nigeria. He'd been approached, he said, by the government there, who wanted him to form a company to develop and build housing estates and factories and schools. Shinwell said there was a fortune to be made for those who invested in the scheme. We stuck in £25,000 straightaway and a lot more money from the Kray coffers followed that little lot straight down the Nigerian drain. It was another case of us getting involved in something we knew nothing about. We just got out of our depth. It happens.

The only good thing about it was that I had a couple of trips to Enugu, which was the capital of that part of Nigeria. On both occasions I was welcomed by Dr Okpara, who was the prime minister at that time. He drove me around, with his chauffeur, in a battered old Rolls and really wined and dined me. I didn't realize at the time, but it was probably Reggie and me who were actually paying for all this VIP treatment.

Just before the end of my second visit to Enugu Dr Okpara asked me if there was anything I hadn't seen or done that I would like to do. I said yes, I would like a guided tour of Enugu prison. I was only in that place for five minutes and that was enough. It was a stinking hell hole and made Dartmoor look like a holiday camp. I felt really sorry for the poor bastards locked up in there.

Ventures like the Enugu project weren't just a case of a couple of East End villains trying to be flash – there was a method in our madness. I'd read and heard how people like Capone built up a lot of their power because they had friends in high places, namely politicians. Not only that, but they also knew things about certain politicians, things which the politician concerned wouldn't want to get out or fall into the hands of the press – secret love affairs, homosexual liaisons, illegal money deals, and so on. Now Reg and I would never resort to blackmail, but it was always useful to know things about important and influential people, and to mix with them. We knew a lot about a lot of people, things they were terrified we would reveal when we were finally gaoled for life. They needn't have worried, though. That was never the style of the Kray twins.

The other unfortunate aspect of the Enugu business is that it led to what became known as the Boothby affair. Ernest Shinwell had suggested that Lord Boothby, a famous political figure, who had once been the Tory MP for Aberdeenshire, might be prepared to invest a good sum in the Enugu probject. He (Shinwell) had already spoken with Boothby, who had expressed some interest, but he wanted to discuss the whole project with someone else who was investing money to compare notes. So I made an appointment to see Lord Boothby – a meeting which later made headline news when Boothby sued the *Sunday Mirror* for £40,000. I was a reluctant witness at the trial – reluctant only because such publicity would draw unwelcome attention to us from the police and the public.

The *Sunday Mirror* got to hear about my approach to Lord Boothby and then, amazingly, wrote a story about a 'top-level Scotland Yard investigation into the alleged homosexual relationship between a prominent peer and a leading thug in the London underworld'. They claimed the investigation had been ordered by the Metropolitan Police Chief Commissioner, Sir Joseph Simpson. The article also spoke of Mayfair parties 'attended by the peer and the thug', of visits to Brighton with other 'prominent public men', of a 'relationship' between the peer, an East End gangster and some clergymen, and there were also allegations of blackmail. You can imagine the stir that little lot caused.

It was the start of a campaign by the *Sunday Mirror* and the *Daily Express* and other newspapers to try to get the Home Secretary, Henry Brooke, to crack down on us and other London gangs. But none of the papers actually named me – they knew they couldn't prove a word of what they were claiming.

Then *Private Eye* joined in and wrote:

Either the charges are true, in which case the newspapers should have the guts to publish names, whatever the risk of libel. Or they are untrue or grossly exaggerated – in which case they should stop scaring the people with this horror movie of London under terror.

The Krays have been with us for a long time, so have the protection rackets. The question is – why has the subject suddenly become a matter for such grave anxiety?

I have kept all the clippings for all these years and even now I am astonished at the headlines I made.

Henry Brooke, the Home Secretary, was forced to join in and issue a statement. He said: 'The Protection Racket situation in London is less serious than it has been on several occasions in the past.' Well said, sir. Then Lord Boothby himself very bravely wrote a letter to *The Times* about what he called 'a tissue of atrocious lies'. Eventually IPC, the owners of the *Sunday Mirror* and the *Daily Mirror*, apologized and paid him £40,000. Cecil King, the IPC chairman, issued a statement saying: 'I am satisfied that any imputation of improper nature against Lord Boothby is completely unjustified.'

So now the whole world knew about Ronnie Kray, top London gangster. Some of them now believed that I was a homosexual and that I had had a homosexual relationship with Lord Boothby. Let me now – for the first time – make the truth absolutely clear. Yes, I was a homosexual at that time, and for many years afterwards I found greater pleasure in the company of men than in the company of women. No, I did not have any kind of sexual relationship with Lord Boothby. It was strictly a business relationship which later became a friendship – a friendship based on the fact that we had both been so badly smeared by the national press.

Boothby was a good man, an honest man. Some time later, when I was charged by the police with demanding money with menaces from a West End club owner, Lord Boothby asked a question in the House of Lords about why the police had held me in custody for five weeks without trial.

As for myself, I was relieved that people now knew about my homosexuality. I didn't have to hide my leanings any more. I didn't feel any shame then – I don't feel any now. It was the way I was born. There is nothing necessarily weak about a homosexual man – and I believe he does no wrong provided he does not force his attentions on anyone who doesn't want them. I hate people who pick on homosexuals. I hate words like 'queer' and 'poof'. Some time later another gangster called me 'a fat poof' – and he died for it.

But that was in the future. Right now we had more than enough problems to deal with.

The publicity the Krays received at that time undoubtedly helped us towards our downfall. Suddenly we were major celebrities, and suddenly, also, we were right at the top of the Metropolitan Police hit list. Every copper in London who wanted to make a name for himself was on the lookout for the slightest mistake by Reggie or Ronnie Kray.

Reg: 1964–66

The Boothby affair, Enugu and Esmerelda's Barn weren't our only problems in 1964. I also got involved with a guy called Daniel Shay in a spot of protection that went wrong. I went with him to a shop whose owner was withholding some money which he owed. Normally in such cases, if Ron or I appeared, there was usually no problem and the 'misunderstanding' was cleared up. However, on this occasion the law was hiding in the next room and they pounced. I appealed, but got sent to Wandsworth for six months. This was the period that I fell in love for the first and only time in my life, but I will tell that story later (chapter 8).

The police continued to harass us, looking for any excuse to get rid of the threat of the Krays. Ronnie was accused of housebreaking, a ridiculous charge, and the case was dismissed. We were both accused of loitering with intent – again, a good lawyer, a poor case by the police, and case dismissed.

Meanwhile, our protection business was booming. New casinos were springing up all over the place, ripe for the picking. We devised a system of payment based on profit – and some of the profits were bigger than you would imagine. Again, we provided a service. Nothing and no one else was allowed to bother the casinos. Of course, if any casino manager started to play silly buggers or if a rival gang or individuals tried to move in on 'our' casinos, then pressure *would* be applied. Usually the threat of trouble was enough – there was very little violence – but if anyone did try it on they would get hurt. But it didn't happen often and they only did it once.

Other gangs occasionally resented the success we were having and there were attempts to put us out of business. There was a home-made bomb which we returned to the guy who sent it, only rather more successfully than he'd sent it to us. He lost one of his hands. There was an attempt to poison us. That guy had his jaw broken. And some gangsters flew in from Europe thinking they were going to do a bit of business in London. We met them at London airport, exchanged greetings, and they went home on the next flight. No bones broken.

We had what we thought was a good team at that time – all hand-picked villains, not rough diamonds, all with a little bit of class, or so we thought. The best of them all was Ian Barrie, my right-hand man. A Scot who'd come south looking for some action, a smart, tough, good-looking guy, with a scar down his face after an accident with some petrol in the army, he was a perfect minder who remained utterly loyal right to the end. Ron's right-hand man was John Dickson, a close friend of Ian Barrie, who'd travelled down from Scotland with him. He had a mean streak and was a good driver, but we were never 100 per cent sure about Scotch Jack, as he was known, and he was to let us down badly in the end.

So did most of the others who were only too happy to ride with us when the going was good: Ronnie Hart, our cousin, Big Albert Donaghue, Ron Bender and, of course, our own brother Charlie was still involved, though not always on a full-time basis. He sort of drifted in and out. Charlie was good to the end – but most of the others let us down badly.

Things picked up as 1964 ended and 1965 began. We began moving our interests – strictly legitimate ones, I might add – into the provinces and bought shares in clubs in Birmingham and Leicester. We also took over another London club – the Cambridge Rooms on the Kingston bypass. The great Sonny Liston, then heavyweight champion of the world, came to the opening of that. We still loved boxing and boxers were still our favourite people.

We even bought a racehorse for our dear mum. It was called Solway Cross and it cost a thousand quid, but it wasn't very successful. Eventually we gave it away in a raffle.

We'd also, with the help of an associate, devised a nice little line in fraud. It's been called long firm fraud and, put simply, it worked like this: we would register a new company, rent a warehouse, and put in a front man as manager whose job it was to establish good relations with the bank and with suppliers. It would run as a proper business for a while and then, when the bank and the suppliers were feeling nice and trusting, we'd put in maximum orders to the supplier and flog the lot at cut-rate prices. We could clean up well over twenty grand in a single day – and the manager and his staff would be long gone before the supplier realized what had happened. Furniture, TV sets, radios, hi-fis – we'd handle anything. It was a nice little earner while it lasted.

The police never pulled us on that one – but they did try to do us in 1965 for demanding money with menaces from a man called Hew McCowan. He ran a club called the Hideaway in Soho and he claimed we were demanding protection from him. The case went to the Old Bailey and we spent fifty-six days in custody. Eventually we got off and held the biggest party we'd ever had – a huge thrash that went on for two days. Then, like the bloke in the advert for razors, we went out and bought the club which had been the cause of the problem. We changed its name, of course – we called it El Morocco.

It was in Gerrard Street and one of the first entertainers we signed up to do a regular spot was called David Essex. He was a complete unknown in those days – but you could see his great talent even then. Unlike so many of the showbusiness stars who were so keen to be in the company of Ron and me all those years ago, David Essex has never forgotten. Some years ago, when I was watching the TV in Parkhurst one night, David was starring in a show, and at the end of one of his songs he sent his greetings to Charlie, Ron and myself. I am proud that his career started in one of our clubs.

Another star who didn't forget us was Lenny Peters who, with his partner Dianne Lee, had a number one hit with 'Welcome Home'. At the time of our trial for murder one of the papers spoke to Lenny Peters and he told them, 'It was seventeen years of hard slog around the clubs. The Kray twins gave me work when I needed it and didn't have it. They let me play at the Cambridge Rooms night club, at Kingston, in Surrey. I speak as I find. Whatever they may have got up to, they were always good to me.' Thanks Lenny. So you see, there are people who've got something nice to say about us. No one can be all bad.

1965 also produced the wedding of the year in the East End. I married a beautiful and lovely girl called Frances Shea, whom I'd been courting for some time. She was the sister of a friend. It was an amazing wedding, packed with celebrities, and one of the happiest days of my life. We went on honeymoon to Athens. At the time it seemed that nothing could spoil my future happiness. But when you start to feel like that life has a habit of kicking you in the teeth.

The underworld grapevine began to warn us about two coppers – Nipper Read and Fred Gerrard. Leonard Read was a chief inspector working out of West End Central Police Station, along with Gerrard, who was a chief superintendent. The word was that Read and Gerrard were making more than the usual number of inquiries about us and were trying to talk to people we'd been involved with in various dealings. It was said that they were compiling a dossier on us and that Scotland Yard had been told by top people in the government that we were becoming too big and too influential. The word was that Read and Gerrard had been told: 'Get the Krays.'

It was a threat we didn't take seriously enough. In fact, we even bought two snakes, evil-looking bastards they were, and we called them Nipper and Gerrard. We had a lot of laughs in the firm over that, although the bloody things kept on escaping and causing a right old stir. In the end we lost one of them altogether and I think we gave the other one back to the petshop.

We never managed to control the little buggers, and I suppose the same was true of Nipper Read and Fred Gerrard. We underestimated them – or, at least, we underestimated the low levels to which they would eventually sink in a desperate attempt to put me and Ronnie away. Really, in the end, they were as devious as most criminals.

But we always had a lot of respect for them, particularly Nipper Read. He was a good boxer and won the Metropolitan Police boxing championships three times. In our book, anyone who's a decent boxer is usually halfway towards being a decent bloke. We still hold no grudge against Read, Gerrard and the others. It was business, as they say, it wasn't personal. Not on our side anyway.

All in all, apart from the McCowan affair, 1965 was a pretty good year. Business was flourishing, and we had built up a good team. Building up a firm – in the underworld sense – takes a lot of time and patience. There's an awful lot of trust involved. We'd got a good mix – or so we thought.

There were our right-hand men, Ian Barrie and John Dickson. From Glasgow was Big Pat Connolly – as his name implies, a very big, tough man. So was Big Albert Donaghue. I'd once shot him in the foot for an act of dishonesty – after that we were as close as brothers, or so I thought. There were others near the top of the firm who let us down badly – Ronnie Bender, Cornelius (Connie) Whitehead, and our cousin Ronnie Hart.

Hart was another strong, good-looking bastard, who loved the glamour of being with us. He came knocking on the door at Vallance Road one day and said, 'Hello, I'm your cousin. I want to join your gang.' We'd never met him before but our checks showed that he seemed to be reliable – another mistake – and so we took him on. He was our cousin but he had the habit of calling us both 'uncle'.

Later a pair of Greek brothers, the Lambrianous, were close to us. Then there was Mad Teddy Smith, a very funny although quite lethal guy from London, and plenty of other fringe members, like Billy Exley, an ex-lightweight boxer whom Ronnie used as a bodyguard occasionally. Exley was a fairly insignificant character in our story in those days but later was the first one to rat on us. But, of course, we had no knowledge of that at the time.

Nor did we have any idea that 1966 was going to be such a dramatic and traumatic year for us. It was the year when we freed Frank Mitchell, the so-called Mad Axeman, from Dartmoor. What we did, though I say it myself, was brilliantly clever. We were tried for the murder of Mitchell, though the police never found a body which is probably why we were acquitted and the case remains open.

1966 was not a good year for Ron's health, which had been very much up and down for some time. He would have good periods when he was his real self – a nice, gentle man fully in control of every situation, who would only get nasty when he was provoked. At other times, though, he would go into deep depressions and disappear for days and weeks on end. He was convinced the police or other villains were closing in on him.

These times put a great strain on me because it left me to run the firm by myself, and I was having plenty of problems of my own in my personal life. Frances was also suffering periods of great depression.

47

Our marriage was going through a bad patch and I was worried about her.

1966 was also the year when our feud with the Richardson gang came to a head. They attacked a club at Catford because they thought some of our gang were inside it. Unfortunately for them, there were a lot of tough customers inside having a drink, but only one member of our firm, a really nice guy called Richard Hart. Hart, who was only thirty, was shot dead. It was senseless. Most of the Richardson gang, including Frankie Fraser, got shot or stabbed. Most of them got put away. The only one to wriggle out of the net was – yes, you've guessed it – that evil bastard George Cornell. So the next night Ronnie killed him. He shot him in the Blind Beggar pub. Ron tells the full story of what happened in chapter 4.

You could say that 1966 was the beginning and the end for the Krays. It was the beginning of the period where we were one of the most feared gangs in Europe. But in a sense it was the end as well, because the government and Scotland Yard could no longer ignore us. Everyone in London was talking about us. It was getting to the point when either the police had to break us or we would have broken them.

It was a pity really. Everything would probably have been OK; we could probably have lived fairly peacefully alongside the law, but for George Cornell and those Richardsons.

Ron: 1966–67

The Richardson affair, which I talk about in chapter 4, cost us our deal with the Mafia – a deal we had been prepared to cut the Richardson gang in on. It was my idea to try to establish links with the Mafia. We knew that some London clubs were funded by them. We wanted to get them to fund more clubs, in partnership with us, and in return we would offer them complete protection from the law and other gangsters. This, we thought, would just be the start. Once the Mafia could see we were to be trusted, they would want to increase their business links with us. With their backing and money and our knowledge and control of the London scene, I didn't see how we could fail.

The problem, initially, was making the right contacts and I thought it would make a good impression if I went to them with our proposals. I didn't know anyone over there, I wasn't sure who I wanted or needed to talk to, so I suppose, looking back, it was either a brave or a bloody stupid thing to do. Talk about walking into the lion's den.

The first problem was getting a visa to get into America – after all, I did have something of a criminal record. Eventually I became involved with an American called Alan Cooper, one of those sort of international Mr Fix-its. You pay him the money and he gets you what you want – in my case, permission to get into America and stay there for a few days. Cooper had a lot of connections and finally he said it was all fixed.

We went first to Paris, where Cooper took me to the American Embassy. He acted as though he owned the place and started giving some woman official a real cock-and-bull story about who I was, how I'd been badly treated by the police in Britain, and how I desperately needed to get into America for a few days to see a sick and dying relation. It worked. She said to me, 'I can see you have got convictions but, under the circumstances, we can grant you permission to visit America briefly.'

We flew to New York and when we landed at Kennedy airport the FBI were there to meet us. They searched us and our luggage very thoroughly and asked me what I wanted in America. I told them the same cock-and-bull story and they told me to report to the embassy the same day. This I did and, despite my convictions and despite the lies we had told, I was allowed into America for seven days.

Cooper took me to meet Joe Kaufman, an Italian-American Jew, who was the Mr Fix-it on the American side. Kaufman had been in London several times and knew who I was. He listened to what I wanted and suggested that we go to Brooklyn to meet Frank Ileano, one of the top men in the New York Mafia. Phone calls were made and a meet was arranged at a house in President Steet, in Brooklyn, owned by three gangster brothers, the Gallos – Joe Gallo, known as Crazy Joe, Larry Gallo and Al Gallo, who for some reason was called Kid Blast.

The atmosphere was electric. I suddenly knew I was in the big league and I'd better make out a good case for being here, otherwise these bastards were liable to chop my balls off. They were deliberately trying to unnerve me, trying to see how much bottle I'd got. Things weren't improved when, as I struggled to make polite conversation, a tiny thickset dwarf came and stood behind my chair. He was carrying a bottle which he held near my head. This evil-looking midget, who I learned later was known as the Dwarf, was Armando Ileano, the brother of the gangster I was waiting to meet. When I saw Armando the Dwarf hovering behind me with a bottle in his hand, I couldn't help thinking of the old saying, 'Mark well the man whom God has marked.' Funny the things that go through your mind when you're quietly shitting yourself with fear.

Frank Ileano eventually arrived. They called him Punchy because he'd been a very good middleweight boxer. He was a most impressive man. Kaufman introduced me and told him that I had got my button, American Mafia slang for murder or murders. He told him he could check me out with Angelo Bruno, a Philadelphia gangster who had knowledge of the London scene. Frank Ileano said, 'Don't worry, I will do.'

He went into another room to phone and after what seemed like an age he came back and said, 'I've checked you out. Bruno says you are OK.' Suddenly the tension in the room began to lift. Out came the coffee and discussions began almost immediately, discussions that covered the club scene in London, the possibilities of bringing big-time American gamblers from Las Vegas to London for week-long orgies of gambling, plus the inevitable subject of drugs and the shifting of them, both in and out of Britain.

Ileano and I got on fine. That night he took me to his club in New York, the Mousetrap. He told me I was very hot and that the FBI were watching me all the time and, presumably, reporting my every move back to Scotland Yard.

Frank Ileano and I continued our discussions over the next few days and I have little doubt we were well on the way to forming a link between the Mafia and the Krays. All in all, it was a highly successful trip and, loaded down with gifts, I returned to London well pleased.

It wasn't long before the Americans showed they were serious about our discussions because one of their top front men – I shall call him John Smith, because he is still in business – arrived in London to talk further business. We met him at the Pigalle with the Richardsons, who by now were getting really troublesome and threatening to disrupt the plans Reg and I were making. So we thought it was better to include them in discussions, rather than have them blow up the Pigalle while we were sitting in it. I tell you, these were troubled times.

Unfortunately Smith and the Richardsons didn't see eye to eye on one point and one of the Richardsons started swearing at him.

I was annoyed at this and said, 'There's no need for the swearing at him. He's in the country on his own.' I could see Smith was pleased at this and we managed to sort out the business to suit all of us.

The next night I took Smith up a tie and handkerchief set.

Some months later I was back in New York, drinking in a bar with the boxer Rocky Graziano, when a man who was obviously a hood approached me. 'I have got a message for you from someone upstairs,' he said.

'Who is it?' I asked.

He said, 'John Smith. He sends you his best wishes. He can't come down to see you because the place is crawling with FBI.'

I thought to myself it was just as well I'd been nice to him while he was in London. After all, now I was very much on his territory.

The American Dream never quite came off for Reggie and me, although we did do some business with the Mafia, but nowhere near as much as we might if things had worked out differently.

Our American links produced other side effects – some good, some bad. The good? Well, one gangster I was chatting to in America told me that the great boxing champion Joe Louis had fallen on hard times. He asked if I could fix him up with a little trip to England. So I rang two brothers I knew called Levy, who ran a club in Newcastle called La Dolce Vita. They were marvellous. They sent Joe Louis first-class air tickets, had a car waiting for him at Gatwick airport, and then paid him more than a thousand pounds for four days of personal appearances, in which all he had to do was say a few words and sign a few photographs.

Marvellous blokes, the Levys. When Reg and I were in Brixton awaiting a demanding money with menaces charge, they sent someone down with a gift of £5000 to help us.

The bad side of the American business were our two main contact men – Alan Cooper and Joe Kaufman. When Cooper first offered to fix up my trip to the States I thought of the old saying, 'Beware of Greek gods bearing gifts.' But I badly wanted to go to America so I ignored my warning thoughts. But my premonitions were proved right because a few months later he was a prosecution witness against us at our trial.

The police also arrested Joe Kaufman and told him they were going to charge him because of his links with us. Kaufman, like Cooper, offered to do a deal with the police: he would tell them everything he knew about the Krays if they would drop the charges against him. Yet another case of rats deserting a sinking ship. We let Cooper get away but at least Reggie had the satisfaction of breaking Kaufman's jaw when we were on remand together at Brixton.

I haven't seen Frank Ileano for many years now. The last time I saw him I gave him a diamond ring worth £1000.

Reg: 1967–68

After the visit to London from New York of John Smith, we got a message that Angelo Bruno wanted to come to London to see us. Bruno was a Mafia godfather from Philadelphia, a very big man indeed in American crime.

We booked him into an hotel in London, along with Rocky Marciano, the former world heavyweight boxing champion, who was a close friend of Bruno's and a useful cover – Bruno would say he was accompanying Marciano on a trip to London, instead of it being the other way round. Also with them was Bruno's minder, Eddie Pucci.

Pucci, a Sicilian-American, we had met before. The Mob had sent him over with the son of a prominent entertainer who was worried

Left and below left: In Bethnal Green where we grew up to be fighters *(Artlem/Mirror Features)*

Below: With our Mother, Violet, in the back yard at our house in Vallance Road

Above: The yard behind our house in Vallance Road

Right: A rare picture of the three of us, Reg, Charlie and Ron, around 1964

Below: Around this time we'd got involved in the scrap business!

Our mother, Violet, holding a toy made by Ron in Broadmoor.
(News of the World)

Above: Vallance Road went mad after our acquittal from the Old Bailey in 1964

Below: A special evening in June 1964. Christine Keeler is seated next to Ron at the Society Restaurant

At the Astor Club. Among our guests are Malcolm Allison and Derek Ibbotson, seated next to Reg

Paul Raymond, Lita Roza, the singer, and Ron

Ron with boxer Billy Walker. *(Halifax Photos Ltd)*

Mum (second right) and Dad (far left, top row) liked a night out. Some of our friends here are Barbara Windsor, Jack Mullins and his father, Dodger Mullins

More of our friends from showbusiness. This group includes Barbara Windsor, Ronnie Knight (next to) Lita Roza, George Sewell, Victor Spinetti and Ronald Frazer

Reg, Ted Kid Lewis and Sophie Tucker at The Talk of the Town (now Stringfellows)

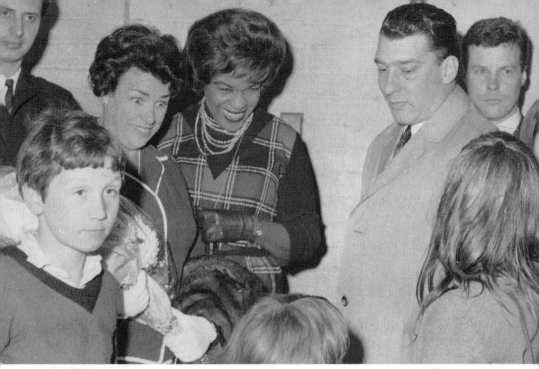

Above: It wasn't all self-indulgence. We were heavily involved with charity work for boys clubs in the East End. Winifred Attwell visited a Bethnal Green youth club with us

Below: The racehorse we bought for our parents never came good and was finally raffled for charity

The great Sonny
Liston signing
autographs at our
club, 1965. *(Halifax
Photos Ltd)*

Sonny again, with the
two of us and Terry
Spinks

Freddie Mills was a
great friend. Here we
are with him, Teddy
Smith, Mickey
Forsythe, John
Davies, Dickie
Morgan and Sam
Leaderman

Mother, George Raft
and friend at the
Colony Club

about the kid's safety. In fact, there was so much concern about this young man that we were actually asked to make sure that he was minded for twenty-four hours a day. Apparently his father's own connections with the Mafia meant that he was a potential target for other criminal organizations.

Our meetings with Bruno took place at the Hilton Hotel. Bruno was very security-conscious and every time we started talking he would get Pucci to turn the radio on in case the room was bugged.

Bruno was said to be a very violent man, but we found him extremely quiet, thoughtful and respectful. When we met for the first time there was an old Jewish gambler in the room, a man Bruno had met many years before and had asked to see again when he was in London. We were all talking and I took my cigarettes out and offered them round. I offered Angelo Bruno a light first of all, but he said, 'Give it to the older man first.' This is just an example of the quiet way he had.

Bruno was very protective about his family, friends and those who worked for him. If anyone did anything to upset any of them, the unfortunate culprits always got the same message: 'If you kick the dog,' he would tell them, 'you kick the master.' Then he would deal with them according to the severity of their crime.

We got on well with him and were on the way to setting up several deals when two things happened: the law moved in on us and death moved in on him. He was slain by gunmen while sitting in a parked car in Philadelphia. We were sorry to hear that.

We were also sorry when Eddie Pucci bought it shortly after we were arrested. Ron had just sent him a bull terrier as a gift, something he'd said he'd like when we'd last seen him. We got on with Pucci particularly well because he shared our love of late-morning drinking sessions. Pucci was shot dead on a golf course in Chicago. And they thought England was a violent place at the time.

Sadly, 1966 had ended so violently, with Cornell and the Richardsons, that the Mafia's interest in doing big business with us seemed to cool off a little. They weren't stupid, they could see what was going on in London – and they wanted to be sure that Ron and I were big enough to ride the storms. We, of course, had no doubts. By

1967 we were also doing business with the Canadian Mafia, in the shape of a man called Don Ceville.

Early that year a large amount of money, in the shape of bearer bonds, had been stolen from banks in Ontario and Montreal. These bonds were really hot in the States and Canada and we were asked if we could dispose of them through our European connections – for a nice percentage, of course. We managed to launder some of this money via financial contacts in London and Paris.

It was a whole exciting new world for Ron and me. Suddenly we could see a different direction to go in. We'd enjoyed the clubs, the spielers, the protection and all the rest of it, but suddenly we saw that there were other, more lucrative, less physical ways of making a bob.

But then, just as suddenly, things began to go very, very wrong indeed. First of all, I lost my wife Frances in June of that year. It nearly bloody finished me. It was a blow from which I never really recovered. I loved my wife. With Frances gone I seemed to lose interest.

To make matters worse, Ronnie's health was going downhill again. All his life, in his bad times, when his head was bad, he'd suffered from terrible depressions and rages. But always my brother Charlie and I could deal with him. Now it seemed to be getting more and more difficult. To tell you the truth, I felt at times I was going crazy myself. And all the time we were aware that the police were increasing their watch on us. We couldn't even go and have a quiet drink in peace.

Then, finally, it got to me – I snapped. I got very drunk one night and was told a man called Frederick had been saying nasty things about Frances and the way I'd treated her. I couldn't take it. I got a gun and had two of the boys take me to the flat where I knew Frederick lived with his wife and kids. It was a mad, crazy scene. I smashed my way through the door into his flat, there was a lot of cursing and shouting, then I shot Frederick in the leg. It could have been his head for all I cared. I just lost control. As it happened it was in the leg and he wasn't seriously injured. A doctor who was on the firm's payroll took care of him. But that episode put more pressure on us.

Then came our rows with a member of the firm called Jack 'The Hat' McVitie (see chapter 6). He was a thug, a hardman we used on a number of occasions, normally when we needed a little pressure applying to someone. But McVitie was drinking too much and taking drugs and becoming unreliable. Not only was he scamming us, he was actually boasting about it as well. McVitie had to be dealt with severely. I killed him, I stabbed him to death. At any other time in our lives maybe I wouldn't have killed him, just hurt him. But this was a bad time for us, a pressure time, so I killed McVitie. It cost me dear.

At about the same time one of our closest friends and another member of the firm, Teddy Smith, disappeared without trace. He simply felt the heat was being turned on, got frightened and did a bunk. Later we learned he went to Australia, which is where I think he still is. But the muckspreading really started and we were suspected of murdering him. Not true. But, like all muck, some of it sticks. Other members of the firm began to worry, wrongly, about their own safety. The time was right for Nipper Read to strike, and he did.

We had seen the signs, of course. Suddenly people who had always wanted to be with us weren't around any more, the likes of Scotch Jack Dickson, Ronnie Hart, Albert Donaghue and others. They just ran away. We thought that they'd simply done a bunk, like others before them, that they hadn't got the balls to tell us outright that they wanted to leave. In fact, it was far more sinister than that. One by one, the police, in the shape of Nipper Read, had got at them. Deals were being done all over the place. 'You tell us about the Krays and we'll make sure you get protection and an easy time in court. And don't worry about afterwards – we'll make sure you get clean away.' A despicable way for any police force to act, but it was the only way they were ever going to nail us.

The trial and the traitors we talk about later (chapter 7). But give them their due, the police did their job well – they knew they had one chance and they took it. If they had failed, the Krays would have been as unbreakable as we thought we were.

Ron and I had made two mistakes. First, we did our own dirty work. We killed two men. A Mafia boss would never kill – he'd always get one of his button men to do it for him. Angelo Bruno once said to us, 'Never get shit on your own hands.' And he was right. We always wanted to lead by example, to show the others that we weren't frightened to get our hands dirty. It doesn't matter that the people we killed were worse than vermin – we should never have done the job ourselves.

Second, we trusted too many people. We made it too soft for them. We took blokes on trust and gave them a good living and some great times. We expected loyalty in return. And that's where Nipper Read screwed us. He realized what we seemed to have forgotten. That, basically, most people are a bunch of shits. With most people it's self first, self middle and self bloody last. And, when the crap hits the fan, it's every man for himself.

We showed loyalty to our men all the way through. But when the heat was on they deserted us and ratted on us – virtually every one. That's why the Krays went down.

We knew the net was closing in on us. We could have tried to run but we didn't. Why? Because, in all honesty, we didn't think we would go down. We underestimated the cunning and the cheating of the police. And even if we did go down, how could we have possibly guessed that the penalty would be so unbelievably monstrous?

But what the hell. At least we reached the top of the pile. We've seen and done things most ordinary guys could only dream about, met people and felt excitement most people never get the chance to feel.

The end came for Ron and me at around six o'clock on the morning of 9 May 1968. We'd decided on a real old knees-up the night before to try to forget our troubles. Ron was in a good mood but I really had the blues. But it was a good night. We went drinking in a pub called the Old Horns in Bethnal Green Road, then we moved on to the Astor Club. We stayed there until five in the morning, that's how good a night it was. Ron had a companion with him, a young man, and so did I, although my companion was of the female variety. No woman had ever replaced Frances in my life but every man needs a little company every now and then.

We went back to Ron's flat at Cedra Court, in Walthamstow, and had just got into bed and were starting to doze off, when the front door came flying off its hinges and the place was jam full of coppers, led by Nipper Read. They stuck handcuffs on us and Nipper made the usual arrest statement. We didn't pay much attention. Being arrested wasn't a shock – we'd been expecting it for a long time. We still thought we'd beat the rap, but if we didn't it was just a matter of guessing how many years. Not too many, we thought, and then we'd be free men again. Little did we know.

As London woke up on that sunny May morning in 1968 and two sleepy gangsters were driven at record speed to Scotland Yard, we knew only one thing: the party was over, but it had been fucking great while it lasted.

3

Reg: The Swinging Sixties

Show business stars have always been attracted to the underworld. I've had many dealings with showbiz stars over the years – some pleasant, some not so pleasant. Let me tell you about the night when Richard Harris, the actor, very nearly got himself killed.

Just before my arrest in 1968 I invited the photographer David Bailey and one of his top models at the time, Penelope Tree, to a party in the East End. David was a very close friend and had taken some wonderful photos of Ronnie and me. I once asked him what his favourite hobby was and he replied simply, 'Sex'. David and Penelope and I then went on to the opening of a new club in the King's Road, Chelsea. David had also invited Francis Wyndham, the writer, and Duffy, another top photographer.

We were having a very pleasant evening, apart from the fact that the next table was occupied by Richard Harris and his friends. Harris was obviously very drunk and began making derogatory remarks about me. He seemed to be getting a kick out of trying to cause a scene, but I did not react. This really got him wild and he began to get very aggressive in his comments. It seemed like he was trying to provoke me into hitting him. But I realized there was no point – I knew he was drunk and I also knew that if a brawl started it would be me who ended up sitting in the dock, the villain of the piece. And no doubt some of the papers would have made him out to be some sort of hero for putting me in my place.

I allowed for the fact that he was drunk, I realized that I had nothing to prove, and I reminded myself that Harris was merely an actor and not a face from the London underworld who was trying to undermine me. If it had been another face then he would very quickly have been sent packing. As it was, I stood Harris's ramblings for as long as I could, then I left, but not before I sent him a short note. It said: 'Dear Mr Harris, Just thank your lucky stars it was me you picked on tonight, and not my twin brother Ron. Yours, Reg Kray.'

It must have had the desired effect. Harris later tried to make up for his awful behaviour by sending me a signed photo and a nice message.

Many people claim to know us whom we've never met. I saw an article recently in which Christine Keeler, the lady at the centre of the Profumo scandal, allegedly said she had been a close friend of ours. Well, I have met Christine on a couple of occasions – once at the Grave Maurice pub in Whitechapel and once at the Society Restaurant, in the West End, and I think she is a very sexy lady. But though she may have brought down a government and befriended a politician, she certainly wasn't very close to the Kray twins.

Her friend in bondage, Mandy Rice-Davies, also seems to write occasional articles talking about her friendship with Ron and me. Well, Mandy, we've never met, but why not come on up and see me some time?

Max Bygraves is another who has talked publicly about things involving Ron and me that have never happened. He once told the press that Ron and I had sat in his audience 'like a couple of dummies'. He said we'd sat there looking menacing and refusing to applaud.

Sorry, Max, we may look like dummies, but neither of us have ever been to see you perform. Nor, I hasten to add, would we wish to. You go on making money, old pal, and good luck to you, but not at our expense, OK?

I've also been hounded for years by people claiming to be related to me in one way or another. In August 1986 the *Sun* newspaper ran a headline which said: 'Reggie Kray is my father'. In the article a bloke called Chris Woodward claimed his mother – a Margaret Richardson – had had an affair with me in the sixties, and he was the result. He also said that as he now had a son, I had a grandson.

I wish it were true. His mother claims that she was one of the firm's molls (groupies) in the sixties. She may well have been – there were always plenty of women hanging around. But she certainly wasn't involved with me personally.

59

She said in the article that she had finally decided to reveal our affair 'in a bid to win freedom for Reg after all these years'. It was a nice thought but a bit late in the day.

Not many folk know it, but during the mid-sixties I actually had dancing lessons. I was trying to improve my social graces so I went to a dance school in the Tottenham Court Road. It was run by the Clark Brothers who, at the time, were ranked among the world's greatest tap dancers. They first came to this country to appear in a Royal Command Performance. At that time they were not nearly so well known over here as they were in America. Ron became a friend of theirs and we organized a big party for them at the old Queen's Hall in Commercial Road to make them feel at home. Many celebrities attended, which really showed how far Ron and I had travelled from the backstreets of the East End. There was Tom Driberg, the MP, who was a regular customer at many of our clubs, and Joan Littlewood and many other stars, including some great boxers – Len Harvey, Ted 'Kid' Lewis, the former welterweight champion of the world. Even in his late seventies, Ted would still come and show us his amazing technique on a punchball in the backyard at Vallance Road. The former featherweight champion, Terry Spinks, was also at the party. Terry was a genuine little fellow who, like so many other fighters before and since, spent his money far quicker than he earned it. But the one thing he never lacked was friends.

We were very close to the Clark Brothers in those days and when they went to Blackpool to appear for a season we stayed at the huge house they had rented in the St Anne's area. They were happy times but, sad to say, once Ron and I were in trouble and got put away, we never heard another word from the Clark Brothers.

The great Sophie Tucker was a star we were very close to. Ron was really her favourite and she would phone him from all over the world. Whenever she phoned Ron would play her a recording of her singing 'My Yiddisher Mama'. It was his favourite song.

Judy Garland was another friend, and also Stubby Kaye who used to write to me in prison. It was through Judy Garland that I met the Beatles. Judy and I were going together to the Establishment Club, and as we walked in we bumped into the Beatles. Judy knew them all and made the introductions. We spent a pleasant time together and I feel, given more opportunity, we could all have become good friends. There's always a bond, a sort of affinity, between people who've come from nowhere and climbed to the top, no matter what business they are in.

Danny La Rue used to frequent the Kentucky Club in the early sixties and performed on the stage there several times. When Danny later had his own club in the West End I often used to go there. Once, after Ron and I had been acquitted of demanding money with menaces after two trials at the Old Bailey, Danny had a field day with a mock trial relating to Ron and me. The audience loved it.

Terry Dene, a top pop singer of the fifties and early sixties, was a close friend of Ron's and often used to stay at the flat Ron had at Cedra Court in Walthamstow. One morning in the early hours Terry arrived quite drunk and, getting no answer from the doorbell, began climbing the drainpipe to Ron's bedroom on the second floor. The caretaker thought we were being burgled and called the police. These days Terry has turned to Christianity and we wish him happiness in his new life.

Billy Daniels was another we were very fond of – a great entertainer, famous for his version of the song 'That Old Black Magic'. Daniels came to see me in Parkhurst on several occasions – maybe because he remembered that I once saved him from a severe beating.

Billy's big failing was his drinking. He would drink a lot and then become very aggressive. Before he started drinking he would be a sweet, gentle man, but after a few drinks he would imagine he was a gangster. On one occasion in the early sixties, in a London hotel, he got a bit aggressive with an ex-boxer, a former heavyweight called Tommy Brown. Brown used to be called the Bear and he could easily have broken Daniels's jaw with one punch. He was just about to when I intervened and managed to quieten things down. The following evening Billy Daniels missed a performance at the Palladium in order to come round to the Kentucky Club and apologize to Tommy Brown and myself. He also gave me a pair of cuff-links as a further gesture of goodwill. Billy knew how close he'd come to a damn good hiding. He also knew who'd saved his bacon.

It's said that on one occasion in New York he was even closer to trouble. He had offended Crazy Joe Gallo, the Mafia boss whom Ron later met. Daniels had been going out with a beautiful air hostess but did not realize that she was one of Gallo's regular girlfriends. Billy was summoned to a tenement basement in downtown New York where Crazy Joe used to keep a caged lion. He would let the lion attack anyone who displeased him. Billy apologized profusely, on his knees at one stage. Gallo let him off on condition that he never saw the girl again. Billy told me later that he never felt the same way about air hostesses – or lions – after that.

George Raft was a man Ron and I had admired in films when we were kids. Little did we think that many years later we would become his friends. We first met him at the Colony Club in Berkeley Square. He was aged about seventy-two then, and I have never seen a more smartly dressed man. He told me that he used to have one meal a day, a steak with salad every evening. He never smoked or drank. We took him around the East End and south London and he met our parents on several occasions. Shortly before he died he gave Ron and me a gold cigarette lighter each. He was a wonderful man.

It was George Raft who introduced me to Robert Ryan, whom I came to regard highly as an actor and as a man. I was with Ryan one night in the Colony Club when we were interrupted by Don Ceville, from the Canadian Mafia, who was over here hoping to do business with us. Ceville was an arrogant man and seemed very put out that Robert Ryan couldn't recollect a meeting they'd once had in America. Hardly surprising when you think that an actor like Ryan must meet thousands of people every year. Ceville actually got quite nasty and I wondered if I was going to have to intervene, but Ryan handled the situation superbly, with great tact and diplomacy. Ceville eventually got the message and drifted away. I heard later that he had been gunned down in Toronto. I must say I wasn't surprised. With his approach to life he was bound to come to a sticky end.

While I'm talking of friends I must mention Diana Dors and her husband Alan Lake. How sad that she should die and he should follow her in such tragic circumstances.

I first met Diana in the early sixties when Frances, who was then my fiancée, was dining with me at the Room at the Top in Ilford. We were both enthralled by this dynamic young singer and actress with the platinum blonde hair.

Diana became a good friend, in every sense of the word. We went out together many times, and when we were put away she would visit Ron, Charlie and me. Not only that, she would go round to see our parents in Vallance Road and make sure they were OK. She never went empty-handed. She always took them gifts and fruit and flowers. She was a bloody wonderful woman with an amazing zest for life, far more pure than her image and the media indicated, a woman with strong values and opinions, and devoted to her husband Alan and son Jason.

Alan, like us, suffered from what you might call a bad press. He was never the wild man the gutter press made him out to be. He was a kind, gentle bloke and a bloody good actor.

When I was at Parkhurst in the early days of the seventies I became friends with a con called Steve Tully, with whom I later became involved in a book about East End rhyming slang. Steve said he would like to meet Alan, so I wrote and asked him if he could come and see me. But the letter was intercepted by the governor, who told me that because I was a Category A prisoner I was allowed only to see visitors that the authorities thought I should see – and Alan Lake wasn't one of them. I demanded an explanation, but never got one, though I suspect it was because Alan had strong contacts in the media and the authorities were afraid he would pass on stories to the papers about me.

To get round the problem, Steve Tully wrote to Alan, got a nice reply, and then sent him a pass to visit him. Steve and I arranged between ourselves that during Alan's visit I would wander across the room to go to the toilet and stop and have a quick word with him, to shake him by the hand and thank him and Diana for their visits to our parents.

Alan travelled all the way down from London – and was then stopped at the main gate and told he couldn't come in. The prison officers agreed that he had an official VO (visiting order), but as he wasn't on Steve's regular correspondence list he couldn't come in. I tell you, there are some hard-hearted sons of bitches around, and they aren't all criminals!

Steve and I were terribly disappointed and thought that Alan would be angry with us. All the time and money he'd spent coming down from London to see two gaolbirds, and then not being allowed in. Worse, being humiliated by a nobody in a uniform at the front door. Imagine our surprise then when we received a lovely letter from him saying how disappointed he was not to see us, how upset he knew we must be – but not one mention of the tiring journey down from London or the inconvenience. That shows you the kind of guy Alan was.

Poor Alan, he found life without Diana unacceptable. Sad, but understandable. It must have been like life without sunshine – and I know a bit about that.

Lenny Peters, the blind singer, I've already mentioned. When he first started, Ron helped him get an engagement at the Blue Angel in the West End and he often appeared at our clubs. Lenny has never forgotten and has even organized shows at Broadmoor for Ron and his friends.

Years ago, before I got put away, whenever I went into a pub or club or restaurant where Lenny was, he would always sense my presence in the room the moment I entered.

I can still remember a big charity night at the Cambridge Rooms, which Ron and I owned. Lenny was doing the cabaret and our guest of honour was the former heavyweight champion of the world, Sonny Liston. Now it was almost impossible to make Liston laugh and he was known as Old Stoneface. Yet, as he listened to a special song that Lenny had written about him, Old Stoneface just broke up with laughter. It was a magical moment.

This reminds me of another story about Sonny and Reg Gutter-idge, the boxing writer and TV commentator and a member of a well-known London boxing family. Reg has only one leg. He lost the other during the war and in its place has a leg made of cork. One night he was in a club on the next table to Sonny Liston, who recognized him but couldn't recall Reg's name. He certainly didn't know that Reg had a cork leg. Liston made a few snide remarks about the 'white commentator' and kept on until Reg, who had had enough, suddenly jumped up, picked up a knife and plunged it through his trousers and into his leg (the cork one, of course).

'Go on then, Mr Liston', said Reggie, 'you think you are tough – you stick a knife in your leg.'

Sonny Liston almost went white. Later Reg revealed his secret and he and Liston became friends. In fact, whenever Liston saw

Reg he would insist on a repeat performance. In the end Reg had to refuse – he was running out of cork!

Yes, great days and great people. It's often said the sixties were a special time, and it's true. Friends Ron and I made in the sixties are still among our closest friends today.

Among them is Joe Pyle, whom we first met in the Double R. He was a promising middleweight boxer who was arrested for the alleged murder of a fellow by the name of Cooney, who'd been shot dead in the Pen Club near Spitalfields Market. Joe went on trial with others at the Old Bailey, but was acquitted. Today Joe is one of the biggest and most successful businessmen in London.

The last time I was outside with Joe, we had a drink at the Astor Club to celebrate the birth of his son. And these days Joe Junior, as well as Joe Senior, keeps in touch with me regularly.

Ron and I have made so many friends over the years – some good, some not so good, some loyal, some very disloyal. But of all the friends I've made – and this is no disrespect to my brother Charlie – the greatest friend I've ever had has been my twin brother Ron. When I was in Parkhurst I wrote a poem about friendship which I dedicate to him. Ron and I have been through so much, good times and bad, and always that amazing bond has been there between us. And it still will be on the day – God willing – when we are together again as free men.

Friendship

Friendship is
An eternity . . . of sorts
Valueless, unlike money,
A true friendship never aborts . . . his friend
Friendship is,
Stronger than steel,
Steel will break in the end,
But what better bond
Than a true friend?
Friendship is,
Entirely, utterly, selfless,
Helps you straighten out

When you are in a mess,
What more to say?
Friendship isn't words, it's feeling,
Sharing, caring
Understanding and believing!
Friendship's qualities
I can't define,
But I have a friend called Ron
Who's a true friend of mine,
And if you look closely
Ever so closely at Ron
You'll see diamonds and gold
Are . . . as none,
When compared to the friendship
I share . . . with Ron.

4

Ron: The Killing of George Cornell

The Blind Beggar public house in the Whitechapel Road in London's Bethnal Green was not what you'd call an attractive pub. It was a big, ugly building in a very poor part of London. Not the sort of place you'd want to take a lady friend for a quiet drink or a business contact to clinch a big deal. It was simply the kind of pub where the poor people in that part of London would go for a drink to drown their sorrows or to have a bit of a knees-up on Saturday nights and pretend they were feeling happy.

But nonetheless the Blind Beggar will go down in the folklore of the East End for two reasons. First, so the story goes, it was named after a poem written in the seventeenth century and entitled 'The Blind Beggar of Bethnal Green'. It tells how a blind beggar had a really beautiful daughter, but when the blokes who came to court her realized that she was the daughter of a mere beggar, they didn't want to know her. She was beneath them. Then one day along came a young man who fell in love with her. He didn't care that she was only the daughter of a beggar. He married her, and only then did the blind beggar reveal that he was a relation of the rich and powerful Simon de Montfort. The beggar, it seemed, was a rich man himself but didn't want anyone marrying his daughter just for her money. So there was happiness – and money – all round. And the young girl had found true love and, presumably, lived happily ever after. It's the sort of rags-to-riches tale that would thrive in such an area of broken dreams.

The other reason the Blind Beggar pub is part of the East End folklore is because of what happened between a bloke called George Cornell and me. It was in this pub that I shot Cornell dead. It was his death which helped bring to an end the reign of Reggie and me – and it was his death, as well as that of Jack McVitie, which has put us away for so many years. Probably, because of it, I shall finish up in Hell. Like my dear old Auntie Rose once told me, 'Ronnie, love, you were born to hang.'

Yet I have no regrets. Cornell was a vicious, evil man. He lived by the gun and the knife and he deserved to die by them.

I knew from a very early age that I was going to kill someone. It was part of my destiny. And I always had this love of guns. I loved the feel of them, the touch of them, and the sound they made when you fired them.

I had shot one or two other men before I shot Cornell. With the others, though, it was always business and not personal. I always aimed to maim, not to kill.

With Cornell, though, it was different. It had become personal as well as business, and – I make no bones about it – I intended to kill him:

I had known George Cornell for a very long time, right back to when we were both tearaways in the East End. In those days he went under his real name of Myers. He probably changed it later to confuse the police. Even in those early days he was a loner and a really mean bastard. But he left us well alone and we left him alone. There was no point in looking for trouble, especially with someone you knew could handle himself.

We had our first real conversations when we were both in Winchester prison as young men. I was there after my mind had gone funny at Camp Hill, he was there for assault. He already had a long record of violence and had been given three years for slashing a woman friend with a knife. She'd said something out of turn and Cornell had gone for her. He had a very short temper and, as was proved later, he enjoyed seeing other people in pain.

When we were at Winchester he told me that he'd got himself into the pornography business and there was a lot of money to be made in it – not only from selling the stuff but also in blackmailing the weak bastards who had bought it. He said he was looking for a partner, but I told him I wasn't interested.

Years later – and this is not generally known – Cornell and I had another conversation in which he admitted to me that he had killed a man. It has long been a mystery what happened to a London gangster called Ginger Marks, who disappeared around 1962. Cornell told me he had shot Marks 'in the head' in a house in Cheshire Street, a road near our home in Vallance Road. He said he had blown Marks's head clean away. But he wouldn't tell me what he'd done with the body, although he did say he'd got rid of it himself.

Well before that, I can remember Cornell and Marks having a blazing row in a pub called the Grave Maurice. I had stepped in between them as I could see it was getting really nasty. I acted as a peacemaker and got them to shake hands. Cornell told me then that he hated Marks and that one day he would 'blow his head off'. I think Cornell was afraid of Marks because Marks always carried a gun. But Cornell swore to me that he was the man who killed Marks.

When Cornell really began to be a problem for us was when he moved south of the river and joined forces with the Richardson gang. This was run by two brothers, Charlie and Eddie, in conjunction with a man known as Mad Frankie Fraser. The Richardsons ran a highly successful scrapyard in Brixton in south London. They made a really good living from it. But Charlie and Eddie were always fascinated by the low life, by doing deals, by making money, by cheating the system. So they began putting together an army of crooks and hardmen. They were thought to have moved into the protection business and other shady deals. It was said that at one time they owned a mine in South Africa, though, like us with our African dealings, they were cheated out of a fortune. It was also said they owned a bank in Mayfair, though I don't know if that is true. What is true is that they were a mightily powerful and feared organization. Feared because if anyone crossed them the Richardsons were ruthless in their retribution.

Some of the techniques used by the Richardson gang made the Kray twins look like Methodist lay preachers. Whereas we believed that a good thick ear or a punch on the jaw would persuade most people round to our way of thinking, the Richardsons had different ideas. It was claimed that they believed in torture and would torture anyone who got in their way or anyone they suspected had been disloyal to them. Even our guys were scared stiff they'd fall into the Richardsons' hands. None of them went south of the river unless they had to, and then they'd scurry back as quick as they could when their business was finished.

There was a sort of truce between us and the Richardsons, based on the premise that they would stay south of the river and we would stay the other side. But it was always an uneasy truce and I had a gut feeling that something or someone would force us into a full-scale war.

That someone turned out to be George Cornell. He moved south and became the Richardsons' chief hatchet man and torturer. He was extremely well qualified for the job.

We had spies in the Richardson camp and it wasn't long before we started hearing stories that Cornell was stirring things up for us. He kept on at the Richardsons and Mad Frankie to move into our territory and wipe us out for good. That would have made the Richardson gang, along with Cornell and Fraser, the kings of London. It was a situation that we could not tolerate. It was also beginning to affect our own business affairs. We were in the early stages of negotiations with the American Mafia at the time and even they got uneasy because they could smell trouble in the London air.

The trouble might still have been avoided, but then Cornell did the most stupid thing he'd ever done in his life. In front of a table full of villains he actually called me a 'fat poof'. He virtually signed his own death warrant.

It happened just before Christmas, in 1965. We had decided to call a meeting with the Richardsons to try to cool things down. We had already had one meeting with John Smith, a top Mafia man from New York, at which the Richardsons had been present, and that had ended unpleasantly with certain remarks aimed at our American guest. But there had to be some sort of deal worked out with the Richardson gang, otherwise it was obvious that a full-scale gang war was going to start, and that would have done no one any good. So we arranged a meeting at the Astor Club, off Berkeley Square. We went there with two of our right-hand men, Ian Barrie and Ronnie Hart. Charlie and Eddie Richardson were there with Mad Frankie Fraser and the inevitable George Cornell.

It soon developed into a very stormy meeting, mainly over how much of the action the Richardsons were going to get in our dealings with the Americans. We didn't want them to have any, but knew we might have to compromise to avoid any bloodshed. Cornell, of course, couldn't resist sticking his oar in, time and time again, even though it was strictly none of his business. The negotiations were actually between the Krays and the Richardsons – the others were there merely for protection, to keep a watching brief. But Cornell was doing his best to stir things up. He said we were fannying (talking a load of rubbish). Then he did a very stupid thing. In front of all those people – our own men and top men from the other side – he said, 'Take no notice of Kray. He's just a big, fat poof.' From the moment he said it he was dead.

After that meeting the troubles and the aggro really began. It was suddenly all about who were the top dogs in London – who were the real kings of the underworld. It was a test of strength and nerve. A few days after that meeting a car mounted a pavement in Vallance Road and knocked down a bloke who looked and was dressed very much like me. It could have been coincidence, but we didn't think so.. Now we were completely on our guard. We sensed that full-scale war was on the cards.

And do you know what? Despite the fact that the aggro was screwing up our American deals, because the Yanks didn't want to know when they could sense there was trouble in the air, despite all that, I was loving it. This, to me, was what being a gangster was all about. Fighting, scrapping, battling – that's what I'd come into it for in the first place. Don't get me wrong. I didn't want to kill people – I just wanted a bloody good scrap. Just like we did when we were kids.

But in March 1966 the Richardsons went and spoiled it all. They made a complete bollocks of the whole thing. For some reason they launched a full-scale attack, guns blazing, on a club called Mr Smith's in Catford. No one really knows why. We might have had a small financial interest in the club, but nothing heavy, nothing serious. Some said that the Richardsons had been tipped off that Reggie and I and half our firm would be in the club that night, and that was why they hit it. But only one member of our firm was there at the time – a young guy called Richard Hart, who was having a quiet drink. He was an extremely nice fellow, with a wife and little kids, but they shot him dead.

As it happened, the Richardsons, Frankie Fraser, Cornell and the rest of them got more than they had bargained for that night. Mr

71

Smith's was full of gangsters, guys who could really handle themselves, and when the Richardsons burst in with knives and shooters these guys hit back. There was one almighty battle and Eddie Richardson and Frankie Fraser were badly wounded. They were also arrested, along with Charlie Richardson. Typically, the one who slipped through the police net, the snake who slithered away through the grass, was George Cornell.

Richard Hart had to be avenged. No one could kill a member of the Kray gang and expect to get away with it. The problem was, both of the Richardsons and Mad Frankie Fraser were in custody and likely to remain so. That left Cornell. He would have to be the one to pay the price. And, let's face it, who better? All I had to do was find him. The next night, 9 March, I got the answer. He was drinking in the Blind Beggar.

Typical of the yobbo mentality of the man. Less than twenty-four hours after the Catford killing and here he was, drinking in a pub that was officially on our patch. It was as though he wanted to be killed.

I unpacked my 9mm Mauser automatic. I also got out a shoulder holster. I called Scotch Jack Dickson and told him to bring the car round to my flat and to contact Ian Barrie, the big Scot, and to collect him on the way. As we drove towards the Blind Beggar, I checked that Barrie was carrying a weapon, just in case.

At 8.30 p.m. precisely we arrived at the pub and quickly looked around to make sure that this was not an ambush. I told Dickson to wait in the car with the engine running, then Ian Barrie and I walked into the Blind Beggar. I could not have felt calmer, and having Ian Barrie alongside me was great. No general ever had a better right-hand man.

It was very quiet and gloomy inside the pub. There was an old bloke sitting by himself in the public bar and three people in the saloon bar: two blokes at a table and George Cornell sitting alone on a stool at the far end of the bar. As we walked in the barmaid was putting on a record. It was the Walker Brothers and it was called 'The Sun Ain't Gonna Shine Any More'. For George Cornell that was certainly true.

As we walked towards him he turned round and a sort of sneer came over his face. 'Well, look who's here,' he said.

72

I never said anything. I just felt hatred for this sneering man. I took out my gun and held it towards his face. Nothing was said, but his eyes told me that he thought the whole thing was a bluff. I shot him in the forehead. He fell forward onto the bar. There was some blood on the counter. That's all that happened. Nothing more. Despite any other account you may have read of this incident, that was what happened.

It was over very quickly. There was silence. Everyone had disappeared – the barmaid, the old man in the public and the blokes in the saloon bar. It was like a ghost pub. Ian Barrie stood next to me. He had said nothing.

I felt fucking marvellous. I have never felt so good, so bloody alive, before or since. Twenty years on and I can recall every second of the killing of George Cornell. I have replayed it in my mind millions of times.

After a couple of minutes we walked out, got into the car and set off for a pub in the East End run by a friend called Madge. On the way there we could hear the screaming of the police car sirens. When we got to the pub I told a few of my friends what had happened. I also told Reg, who seemed a bit alarmed.

Then we went to a pub at Stoke Newington called the Coach and Horses. There I gave my gun to a trusted friend we used to call the Cat and told him to get rid of it. I suddenly noticed my hands were covered in gunpowder burns, so I scrubbed them in the washroom. I showered and put on fresh clothing – underwear, a suit, a shirt and tie. (We had spare sets of 'emergency' clothes at several places.) All my old clothing was taken away to be burned. Upstairs in a private room I had a few drinks with some of the top members of the firm – Reg, Dickson, Barrie, Ronnie Hart and others. We listened to the radio and heard that a man had been shot dead in the East End. As the news was announced I could feel everyone in the room, including Reg, looking at me with new respect. I had killed a man. I had got my button, as the Yanks say. I was a man to be feared. I was now the Colonel.

Later that night we were having a party at a flat we owned in Lea Bridge Road, when the Flying Squad came pouring in. We'd been expecting them. After all, by now the whole of London knew who'd killed George Cornell. But, of course, the police had to prove it.

There could only have been four witnesses – the barmaid, the old man and the other two blokes. A representative of the firm had already been to see them all. We were fairly confident that none of them would talk. Over confident, as it turned out a few years later.

I was taken to Commercial Road police station in Stepney and Reg was taken to Leyton police station. I was put in an ID parade. Two men walked by but they didn't pick me out.

Then in came Detective Chief Superintendent Tommy Butler, the man they called the White Ghost, who was later to hunt down all the so-called Great Train Robbers, with the exception of one Ronnie Biggs. He never did nail Biggs though he probably broke his heart and his health in trying. He was disappointed about not nailing me as well. 'It's not over yet,' he said. 'We may want to see you again. We'll be in touch.' But Butler never got in touch and shortly afterwards he must have been taken off the Cornell case. He, like the rest, found the Krays a difficult pair to nail.

I was a free man again. Only now there was a very big difference. I had killed a man, and everyone knew I had killed him, including the police. Now there was no doubt that I was the most feared man in London. They called me the Colonel because of the way I organized things and the way I enjoyed battles. It was a name that I loved. It suited me perfectly.

After Butler had released us, we stayed a few nights with our mum at Vallance Road, but one night Cornell's widow came round and broke some windows and called us 'murderers'. Naturally, our mother was upset. And so, too, was Mrs Cornell. That was why we let her off with damaging our house – something that no one else would have got away with. But we could understand her being overwrought. After all, she'd lost her meal ticket when Cornell went down and she probably did love him in her own way. Of course, Mrs Cornell was told not to come round again, and that was the end of that.

It had been a wearying time, so Reg and I went away for a holiday in Morocco, where we stayed with Billy Hill and his girlfriend, Gypsy. We had a bloody marvellous time over there. Among the other guests were millionaire's daughter Anna Gurber and her husband and the legendary Dandy Kim Waters. We had some wonderful parties and everything was fine until the Moroccan police came knocking on the door and told us to leave because we were 'undesirables'. Obviously Scotland Yard was trying to put pressure on us, but that was all they could do. They had no evidence on the Cornell killing and no witnesses.

Unknown to us, of course, the police eventually did a very smooth job on the barmaid, persuading her to give evidence against us. She was a very silly girl but also a very lucky one. Lucky in as much as we could, with one phone call, have had her marked for life. But Reggie and I never hurt women or kids, no matter what the provocation. We only ever hurt other villains but even they, once we were arrested, were let off. It was as though we suddenly decided enough was enough.

Cornell was dead, the Richardsons and Frankie Fraser were locked up, and the Krays ruled London. Nothing at that stage could stop us. Everyone seemed frightened of us – people were actually ringing up begging to pay protection money!

Since those days Reggie and I have become friends of the Richardsons and Frankie Fraser. In 1969 Eddie Richardson and Reg were both in the special security block at Parkhurst. On one occasion Eddie went on hunger strike with the intention of bringing various complaints he had to the attention of the press. However, though he was officially on hunger strike, Eddie didn't really want to starve, so Reg used to leave hard-boiled eggs for him behind the toilet seats to help stave off his hunger pains. And to think that only a few years earlier they had been such deadly enemies. What might have happened if we could have settled our differences and got together? We could have ruled Europe.

Reg also served time in Parkhurst with Eddie's brother Charlie. They would discuss theories on positive mental attitude and things like that. Frankie Fraser was also at Parkhurst for a time but then he was moved to Broadmoor where he and I became very close friends. Reg and I also have a lot of admiration for Frankie's sister, Eva. She travelled many miles to visit Frankie in various prisons but always found time to write to Reggie and me.

My brother Charlie met Frankie Fraser and the Richardsons socially not too long ago and I was pleased when Charlie told me that, despite the passing of the years, they all looked fit and well. Charlie Richardson was reminiscing about the time when he was in

Shepton Mallett army prison with Reg and me all those years ago. So in the end all that animosity between us and Fraser and the Richardsons was unnecessary because they turned out to be such nice guys. There was just one bad apple in their team – George Cornell – and he upset the apple cart for everyone.

Cornell was unlucky – George Dixon was lucky.

After our problems with Esmerelda's Barn we had taken over a club called the Regency in Stoke Newington. To be honest, it wasn't much of a place, an illicit gambling club, but it made good money for us. It also attracted a fairly unsavoury sort of clientele, the sort with big money, big mouths and big fists. Occasionally I had to lay down the law and stop the worst offenders coming in. George Dixon, I decided, had to be banned because of his heavy drinking, and because I heard he'd been making comments about my sex life, something I always hated. He'd once been a friend but he was pushing friendship beyond the limits. So I barred him. But it made no difference.

I'm sitting in the Regency one night when in comes Dixon. He comes marching up to me, bold as brass, a very stroppy look on his face, and he says, 'What's all this then, Ron boy, stopping me coming in here? What's your game?'

I could never stand being spoken to like that. I thought to myself that I would kill him. So I took a revolver out of my pocket, put it against Dixon's head and pulled the trigger. Nothing happened. It didn't go off. Dixon went white, screamed and ran out of the club. He never came back. I used to have a fellow drive me about, named John, from Canning. I took the bullet that didn't fire out of the revolver and gave it to the fellow who drove me about, telling him to give it to Dixon. I told him to tell Dixon he must have nine lives, like a cat.

Since then I have again become friendly with Dixon and his family and they come to visit me in Broadmoor. I have found them to be good people. I am glad now that Dixon lived.

But I still can't bring myself to have the same feelings about George Cornell. As Charlie Richardson said in a newspaper article recently: 'Cornell showed a lack of respect. He had to pay the price. . . . Respect was what we were all about, like the Krays. When we were put away the real crimewave started. In our day we had no

76

mugging and no local burglary. You could safely leave your front door open when you went out. If anyone did step out of line, they simply got a smack in the mouth.' Our sentiments entirely.

The end of Cornell marked the beginning of the next great Kray coup – the freeing of the Mad Axeman, Frank Mitchell, from Dartmoor. A feat considered impossible at the time. But, after Cornell, we believed that anything and everything was possible.

5

Ron: The Truth about the Mad Axeman

The greatest coup, the most brilliant stunt, ever pulled by the Kray twins, came in 1966, when we managed to free a con known as the Mad Axeman from Dartmoor prison. His real name was Frank Mitchell and he was an extraordinary man – 6 feet 3 inches tall, with huge hands, a dagger tattooed on his left arm, a massive physique, great boxing skills, and a heart of gold. He wasn't mad and he wasn't even a skilled axeman. He got his nickname because once, when he was short of readies, he was said to have threatened some people with an axe so that they would give him money. In fact, although he had the strength to tear two men apart at the same time with his bare hands, he wouldn't hurt a fly – he was truly a gentle giant.

Reg and I felt sorry for Frank because, although his crimes weren't serious, the authorities had locked him away without giving him any date for his release. Furthermore, they had stuck him in Dartmoor, just about Britain's most primitive gaol. I had made a promise to Frank that we would get him out of there, though, to be honest, I never really thought he would take me up on it. But then we received letters from him passed on by friends who visited him, saying how desperate he was getting, how the prison governor refused to see him to discuss his problems, and how he wanted us to help him escape.

That was easier said than done. An escape from Dartmoor seemed a tall order. The prison is set in the middle of some of the wildest and boggiest moorland in the country. Few prisoners have managed to escape from it. Anyway, Reg and I sat down to discuss Frank Mitchell's plea. After a good chat we decided to give it a go. After all, we had made him a promise, and if we could spring him from Dartmoor, it certainly wouldn't do our reputation any harm.

The idea, at that stage, was to spring Frank from Dartmoor, bring him to London and hide him in a secret flat. While he was there we would arrange for letters to be sent to the national papers and the Home Secretary saying that if Frank's case was reviewed he would return voluntarily to Dartmoor. If the authorities wouldn't agree to consider his case, then we would make sure he got away. It was a tall order and, looking back, maybe it was a crazy thing to attempt, but at that time we had so much power and so many powerful people in our pockets we felt we couldn't go wrong.

Reg decided that he would personally recce Dartmoor to see what the prospects were. So he wrote to the governor – using a false name, of course – asking him if he would like a visit by the great ex-boxer Ted 'Kid' Lewis, who would give a talk to the prisoners about his boxing career and show films of his old fights. We hired the films from a film distribution company in Wardour Street. We soon received a letter from the governor saying he would be delighted to meet Ted and was 'thrilled' that Ted would be giving a talk to the prisoners.

A few weeks later Ted and three 'associates' (i.e. Reg and two other East End villains with criminal records as long as your arm) made the journey by road to Dartmoor. Needless to say, Reg and his companions had disguised themselves as much as possible, just in case. Luckily it was raining hard, so they were rushed through the courtyard of the prison and not checked out properly. Eventually they reached the area of the prison where the films were to be shown. The projector and screen were erected and the show began.

The Dartmoor cons loved Ted and gave him a standing ovation. Ted himself wept with emotion – by this time dear Ted was in his seventies.

During the show Reg and the other two 'associates' were sitting in a gallery overlooking the stage and all the cons. They were having a really good look round when some of the cons in the audience recognized them and began waving at them. Frank Mitchell, of course, ignored Reg.

One of the prison warders sitting near Reg turned to him and said, 'Where do you know those blokes from?'

Reg pointed to one of the two villains he'd brought along and said, 'I don't know them at all – but I believe they think he is Norman Wisdom.'

79

'Oh yes,' said the screw, 'yes, even I can see a likeness.'

After the show the governor and the padre took Reg, Ted and the others for a meal. The governor seemed to enjoy telling Reg about the various convicts he'd had under his wing. They even spoke about Frank Mitchell, whom the governor called 'a sad case'. At the end of the meal they all shook hands and the governor asked Reg if he would bring Ted Lewis, or some other great fighter, back to the prison. Reg said he would do his best. He certainly hoped to be back at the gaol in the near future.

I know all this sounds incredible, a figment of my imagination – but it really happened. Mind you, a lot of the things which were happening in Dartmoor at that time were quite incredible.

When Reg came back to London and told me what had happened, we decided that freeing Frank Mitchell was going to be easy. And it would certainly get the country talking.

We weren't quite sure when to pull the job but then, to our surprise, we got a phone call from Frank that made up our minds for us. The call was made to my flat at Cedra Court and Frank said, 'I can't take any more uncertainty, Ron. I must escape. Remember your promise to help me. If you don't help me, I'll break out by myself.'

A week later, on 12 December 1966, two of our top men, Albert Donaghue and Mad Teddy Smith, drove down to Dartmoor on a morning when we knew Frank would be on an outside working party. He slipped away from the other prisoners and when Albert and Teddy found him he was contentedly feeding the moorland ponies. They bundled him into the car and raced him back to London.

There was no need for all the panic – it was *six hours* before Frank Mitchell was missed! It was as easy as that. This didn't surprise us, any more than getting a phone call from Frank. At our trial the landlord of a pub six miles from the prison said that Frank had been in the pub on several occasions and bought bottles of vodka, whiskey and brandy, and flagons of cider. On his last visit, said the landlord, he'd changed notes of five pounds and ten pounds. Even the judge said, 'It sounds like cloud cuckoo land.'

It was also revealed that Frank used to go shopping by taxi to Okehampton, where he would buy budgerigars for other prisoners.

It was on one of these trips that he made his phone call to us. Most amazing of all, perhaps, Frank even had a couple of girlfriends on the moor, and when he wasn't boozing, he would slip away from the prison working party and give them one in the heather. The attitude of the prison officers was, apparently, 'Just keep Frank happy – he's no bother that way.'

If the public realized the extent of the corruption in the prison and police service over the years, they would be amazed. Just before we sprang Frank, a warder working at Dartmoor had been sentenced to three months in prison for taking bottles of scotch and tobacco into the gaol for the cons. The way the authorities picked on him was a joke. At that time half the warders in the British prison service were at it one way or another. And Reg and I used to send booze and tobacco into a good many of Britain's prisons simply to make life a bit more pleasant for our mates inside. After all, what are friends for?

I suppose Frank could have escaped by himself, but he was the sort of person who always needed organizing.

We took Frank to a flat in Barking owned by a friend of ours called Lennie Dunn. We did all we could for him. We provided him with companions, the likes of Teddy Smith, John Dickson and Billy Exley. We provided him with a woman, a big attractive blonde, to attend to his physical needs. This was important because Frank was as randy as a stoat. I've never known a guy like it. He would give a bird one and then give her another one with hardly a pause for breath. Women went wild for him. They'd queue up just to be given one by him. He looked like a gypsy, had a body like Charles Atlas and screwed like a rabbit. It was what you might call a winning combination.

We got Teddy Smith, who was the best writer among us, to write a letter for Frank to the Home Secretary. It said: 'All I am asking is a date of release. From a young age I have not been free. I am not a murderer nor a danger to the general public.'

We posted copies of the letter to the *Daily Mirror* and *The Times*. It was published, and everyone waited for a reaction. If there had been one, if the Home Secretary had been wise enough, humane enough, to say, 'OK, this man's case will, at least, be looked at,' then Frank would have been on his way straight back to Dartmoor. As it was, there was nothing, no response at all. Which meant there was no way that Frank was going to go back to Dartmoor and a future without any hope at all. He appealed to us to help him still further, and we agreed.

Now this was a difficult time for me personally because I was hiding from the law, but not for the usual reasons. Quite the opposite, in fact. The police wanted me to appear as a witness for them against a bent copper who'd been offering us protection and immunity for members of the firm in exchange for money. There was no way I would ever appear as a witness for the police, not even against a rogue cop. It's against all my principles. So I went into hiding at a friend's house in Mayfair, which meant leaving poor old Reg in charge of the whole operation.

Charlie, our brother, wanted to drop the whole thing – to take Frank Mitchell back to Dartmoor and make him give himself up, but there was no way Reg would do that. Neither he nor I regret that decision, even though the whole affair developed into a nightmare. In the end Frank was driven to the farm in Suffolk which we had used ourselves in the past and which we knew was safe. He stayed there for a few days, then was taken by boat to the Continent. After that your guess is as good as mine.

To the best of my knowledge, the Axeman is still alive and well and living in —— I won't reveal where. Perhaps South America, perhaps Australia, maybe even Spain. Certainly not in Britain. I doubt Frank Mitchell will ever be found. It's amazing what a new passport, a change of identity and a bit of plastic surgery can do.

As is now well known, eleven days after we had freed him we were charged with murdering Frank Mitchell. We were tried at the Old Bailey. The prosecution said that Charlie, Big Pat Connolly and I freed Frank Mitchell from prison and that Reg and Freddie Foreman – a London club owner – murdered him. We pleaded not guilty. They also said that Reg had harboured Mitchell. Technically he did, and he pleaded guilty to this charge.

Albert Donaghue told unforgivable lies in court. He said, 'It took eleven or twelve bullets to kill Frank Mitchell. I saw Freddie Foreman pump him full of bullets in a van in Barking.' Freddie Foreman may or may not have been in a van in Barking – a van that may or may not have been on its way to a farm in Suffolk. But

Freddie Foreman certainly did not pump Frank Mitchell full of bullets, and that was the conclusion of the court of law too.

It was said in court that Foreman received £1000 for killing Mitchell, that Foreman and a man called Alfred Gerrard shot him, and that Ronald Oliffe was the driver of the van in which he was shot. Donaghue also claimed he heard Gerrard say, 'The bastard's still alive. Give him another one, Fred.'

The jury considered the case for seven hours and twenty minutes and found us not guilty.

The prosecution had tried, and failed, to prove that we had murdered Frank Mitchell. And despite what countless newspaper and magazine articles and television programmes have said, despite the outlandish claims made by John 'Scotch Jack' Dickson in his book *Murder without Conviction*, despite all the lies and suspicion, I say again: we did not kill Frank Mitchell.

It seems no matter how many time we claim our innocence, some people will always believe we killed him. We've owned up to the crimes we have committed, but I'm buggered if either of us is going to get done for murders we haven't committed. It's been said we kept Frank Mitchell in the van for six days and than chopped up his body, that his brain was remarkably small, that his body was sent to a farm and put in a pot, that he was buried in a motorway flyover, that he was turned into pig food – all the usual things.

Dickson, in *Murder without Conviction*, tells the most extraordinary tales. He quotes me as saying to him, 'He's fucking dead. We had to get rid of him. He would have got us all into trouble.' I deny saying that, and it's interesting to note that Dickson has no witnesses – not one person to substantiate his claim. Dickson also claims to have heard three shots as he sat in the flat when Frank Mitchell got into the van. It's true Dickson was in the flat – he'd been helping to look after Frank. But how strange that he heard three shots, while Donaghue said he heard eleven or twelve shots. Someone somewhere must have been a bit confused. Either that or one of them couldn't count.

Dickson also accuses me of apparently trying to murder him. He says he stayed with me at my flat at Cedra Court after the Mitchell business. He says, 'I eventually dozed off. I was awakened by the smell of gas. The gas fire in my room had been left with the gas switch open. I got up and turned it off. I didn't sleep after that. My mind was working overtime. Did Ronnie come in and turn it on or did I accidentally turn it on? I never found the answer to that one.'

I can tell him the answer to that. Like much of his book, the story comes from his own lurid imagination. I never gassed anyone in my life and if I had wanted to kill Dickson I would have found a safer place than my own flat.

However, to be fair, Dickson does admit in his book that when he quizzed Albert Donaghue – the man who claimed in court he saw Freddie Foreman kill Frank Mitchell – he got nowhere. Dickson admits, 'No matter how persuasive I was, he didn't intend to tell me who he thought shot Mitchell.' He couldn't tell you, Dickson, because, as you well know, Mitchell wasn't shot.

The accusations about Frank Mitchell really hurt Reg and me. We were all very fond of Frank, particularly my brother Charlie, and horrified to be accused of his murder. Charlie even wept in court.

And while I'm about it I'd like to express my feelings about Freddie Foreman – a guy who took his punishment like a man.* He was luckier than we were – they eventually let him out. And I'm pleased to say he seems to be living happily and successfully in Spain. I'm told he's even vice-president of the Marbella Boxing Club. The police still want him apparently, but Freddie is too clever for them. Good on you, Fred.

And as for Frank Mitchell, the man they called the Mad Axeman. He wasn't mad, he wasn't an axeman, and he isn't dead either. Like many others, he has good reason to thank the Krays. One day he will reappear and then the world will know the truth.

* In 1969 Foreman was convicted for disposing of the body of Jack McVitie – see chapter 6.

6

Reg: The Last Supper –
The Killing of Jack McVitie

Yes, I killed Jack McVitie. I denied it at my trial and I've wished ever since that I hadn't. You see, I'm not ashamed of having killed him. I don't believe I had any choice. It was either him or me. In my book, I *had* to kill McVitie.

He was killed for several reasons. He cheated us – not once, but several times. He was becoming a danger – to himself, to the whole system we had built up, and a danger to me personally. He had said publicly on more than one occasion that he wanted to kill me, and I had good reason to believe that it was no idle threat. He'd become crazy, his mind demented by a combination of booze and drugs. So in October 1967 I killed him.

I did not regret it at the time and I don't regret it now, even though the extermination of a man no better than a sewer rat has cost me my freedom for the best part of my life. I have paid the greatest price of all. Hanging would have been preferable to the hell I've been through for the past twenty years. Every day, even now, is a living nightmare. The price I've paid has been totally out of proportion – but still I say I don't regret it.

To understand what I'm saying you have to understand what it was like to be a villain in the East End in the fifties and sixties. It was a jungle, it was survival of the fittest. There were some very tasty guys living up there in those days, guys who were useful with their fists and who weren't averse to using a razor or even a gun. These boys meant business, there was no pissing about. So when you got to the top of the pile, like Ron and I did, people were always trying to knock you off (and I mean 'knock off' in every sense). When that happens, when someone tries to put the frighteners on you, you've got three choices. You either run away, or you stay where you are and let them take what they want, or you get them before they get you. It's the same in show business, or in big business, or in life generally. The only difference is, in the underworld blokes don't die of heart attacks – they get beaten up or cut up and sometimes killed. It happens – it always has and it always will.

It was the same with Jack McVitie. He fancied his chances, he was making very serious threats. In the end it was a case of him or me.

McVitie was a slag (a contemptible person). Ron and I had used him a few times over the years as a heavy. When certain people were getting a bit out of hand we'd send McVitie along to sort them out. We used him as a frightener. When other villains copped a look at him and one or two of our other boys, they'd usually hand over the money they owed or stop doing whatever they were doing which had upset us.

McVitie was tough all right. He once got into a bit of bother with the husband of one of his bits of stuff. This particular geezer took exception, and he and half a dozen of his mates were waiting for McVitie outside a pub one night. They took a crowbar to his hands. Really smashed them up so he wouldn't feel like using them to mess about with women again. His hands were really mangled but it didn't stop him. Within a few weeks he was up to his old tricks.

Women were McVitie's weakness. He had a way with them. I couldn't understand it. He was bald, that's why he always wore a hat, he was no looker and he wasn't a snappy dresser. But he could still pull them – and some of them lived to regret it. He chucked one of his birds out of a car when it was going at forty miles an hour. She broke her back and was in agony, but McVitie thought it was a laugh. The woman was too frightened to complain to the law about what had happened.

On another occasion he razored a guy in a club, cut the guy's face to ribbons, then wiped the blade of the knife on a woman's evening dress. There was blood everywhere and she screamed the place down. McVitie thought it was so funny, he nearly razored her for good measure.

This was the guy I killed. I'm no saint, but Jack McVitie was worse. I only ever hurt other villains and then it was business, never personal. McVitie would hurt anyone and wouldn't give a toss. I killed a dangerous man and got thirty years for it. I accept that no one has the right to go around killing people, but thirty years for killing scum like McVitie? And when my own life was in danger? It's ridiculous.

As I say, women were his weakness. But so too were the booze and the drugs. The booze made him mean and the drugs made him constantly short of money.

Foolishly, after he'd been on the booze all day, I took him with me to collect some money owed to us by a club owner in Stoke Newington. This guy's club had been having a rough time from local thugs, so he asked us for protection. He was getting the protection, but we weren't getting the money. He hadn't paid for several months and owed us roughly £1000. The club owner got in a real sweat, said times had been hard, and could he pay a couple of hundred pounds up front and the rest would follow later. I accepted his explanations, admittedly not very happily, when suddenly McVitie whipped a gun out of his pocket and shot the guy in the foot. He was crazy – the guy was screaming in agony, and if the law had come we'd have both been put away in no time. As it was, I smacked McVitie around a bit until he cooled down and then arranged for a doctor on our payroll to attend to the club owner. He finished up in hospital, of course, and there were questions asked, but, luckily for us, he had the good sense to keep his mouth shut and we, in return, overlooked the money he owed us. But I made a mental note never to take McVitie along with me on a collection again. The man was becoming dangerous. It was only a matter of time before he would kill.

Then there was the job we sent him on in Kent. We offered him £200 to pick up some merchandise from a warehouse in Kent and deliver it to an address in Stoke Newington. He was given fifty quid for expenses in advance. We didn't trust him, so we sent John Dickson, Ron's right-hand man at the time, to trail him.

On the return journey Dickson soon realized that McVitie wasn't heading in quite the direction he should have been. He was obviously calling in somewhere else first with our lorry-load of merchandise. Dickson continued trailing him, but McVitie saw Dickson, realized what he was up to and lost him in the London traffic. Eventually McVitie turned up in Stoke Newington with the lorry, which, of course, was minus some of the stuff it had been carrying.

It was a clear case of double-cross. McVitie denied it, of course. We couldn't prove anything and we weren't into the 'torture and tell' business like the Richardson gang across the river, so we decided we'd let him off – for the time being.

But McVitie was such a prat. Instead of being thankful, he went straight out, got drunk and started telling all and sundry, 'I've just turned the Krays over and they've done bugger all about it. I tell you, they're getting soft. They'll have to watch it.' But he was living on borrowed time. So, too, was the owner of the warehouse in Kent. We were convinced he was involved with McVitie, and after a few threats he owned up.

We still had the problem of what to do about Jack McVitie. He was drinking more and more and taking a lot of really lethal pills – black bombers they were called. Like a fool, I felt sorry for him. He'd done a fair bit of work for us in the past, and Ron and I always showed loyalty to anyone who had worked for the firm.

But then McVitie did a crazy thing. He cheated Ron out of some money he owed on some purple hearts. It was only a hundred quid, but it upset Ron. He felt that if you let one villain cheat you and get away with it, then others would start fancying their chances and start taking liberties. McVitie had cheated us – not once, but twice – and he was boasting about it in the pubs.

As if all this wasn't enough, McVitie got smashed out of his brains on booze in a club in Balham owned by Freddie Foreman. Unfortunately he also caused a very bad scene and started to break the place up. Luckily for him Freddie Foreman was not about, because Freddie is not a guy to mess with. But he was a very good friend of ours and this was really embarrassing – a member of our firm smashing up his club.

Ronnie and I weren't having any more of it. We apologized to Freddie, squared up with him for the damage and sent a message to McVitie to meet us at the Regency in Stoke Newington. Ron really slagged him off over the damage to Foreman's club, and over the missing merchandise and the club owner who'd been shot. Ron was bloody furious and said he wanted the money McVitie owed on the purple hearts, there and then, or else. When Ron was in that sort of mood he'd scare the pants off anyone, and McVitie was scared all right. He told us he owed a lot of money, his nerves were bad, he couldn't get off the pills, his kid was sick and he just didn't know what to do. 'Give me one more chance, Ron,' he kept saying. 'Please give me one more chance.'

Like a bloody idiot I started feeling sorry for him. It was the stuff about the sick kid that got to me. I could never resist a line like that. I didn't know if it was true or not, but McVitie had one or two kids scattered about, so – like a bloody fool – I lent McVitie fifty quid. I should have known he'd blow the lot on booze and pills.

When I later told Ron that I'd slipped McVitie fifty quid he went beserk. He sent a message to McVitie saying he wanted all the money back or else. McVitie must have thought I'd dropped him in it with Ron on purpose, which was a load of bollocks. The silly bastard got drunk again and a couple of nights later he comes into the Regency waving a sawn-off shotgun and screaming he's going to kill 'those fucking Krays'.

Luckily we weren't in the Regency that night, otherwise McVitie would have shot us to pieces. But people who were there said he definitely meant what he said, and he was going to get me in particular.

Now when a guy like McVitie is making threats about you and walking around with a shotgun, if you ignore it, you're asking for trouble. Not only that, all the other villains are looking at each other and saying 'What's happening to the Krays? They're letting this McVitie make 'em look like a right pair of soft prats.' It's a matter of honour, what the Eyeties call 'face'. If you show you're weak, the others start to close in on you like sharks.

We had to make an example of McVitie. Even then I didn't intend to kill him – just to give him a bloody good hiding. So early the next night I went down to the Regency to look for him. I took a gun with me, a .32 automatic, but I didn't intend to use it – not unless McVitie started anything nasty. I'd never shot anyone before, except with a slug gun when I was a kid.

I also took some muscle with me, just in case things started getting rough. There was Ronnie Hart, our cousin, and the Lambrianou brothers. They were trying to get on the firm at the time and were looking for ways to show Ron and me that they were up to it. We were a bit particular about who we took on. The only reason Hart was on the firm was because he was family, and what a mistake that turned out to be. He turned Queen's evidence and it's because of him as much as anybody else that I am where I am today.

McVitie wasn't in the club, luckily for him, so I went for a Chinese meal with Hart and the Lambrianous. Who should be sitting in the restaurant but Jack McVitie – pissed as usual, broke, and bloody offensive. He called me some names and then said, 'I'll kill you, Kray, if it's the last fucking thing I do.' Then he staggered out without paying.

I paid his bill – I didn't want any more fuss. There were a lot of people around, ordinary civilians. But as I paid that bill I remember thinking: that's your last supper, McVitie. I had no doubts that the guy was a maniac and he was trying to kill me. Now I was going to kill him. I'd had just about enough.

We were going to a party that night at a flat in Stoke Newington owned by a girl called Carol. I got there about eleven with Hart and the Lambrianous. Ron was there with a couple of young guys and Ronnie Bender, who'd done a few jobs for us.

Ron was in a bad mood. He sent Carol and her mates away to another flat, and we sent the Lambrianous to find McVitie and invite him to the party. I never thought he would come, I didn't think he would fall for it. He was friends with the Lambrianous, but he also knew they were as good as on our firm. But he was pissed and the thought of getting his hands on more booze and on some birds must have persuaded him. Anyway, he turned up about midnight with the Lambrianous and a couple of other guys in an old Ford Zodiac. He came straight into the flat and said, 'Where's the birds and the booze?'

I took out the gun and tried to shoot him in the head. I pulled the trigger twice. I wanted to get it over and done, but the gun jammed. The same thing had happened before with Ron and George Dixon. Ron took it as an omen and let Dixon go. McVitie thought I'd do the same with him. 'Come on,' he said. 'You let Dixon off.'

'Yes, Jack,' said Ron, 'but we ain't letting you off. You've taken too many liberties.'

It was starting to get confusing. The gun hadn't gone off and I'd had a few drinks myself. I started to struggle with McVitie and Ron was screaming at him, calling him a slag. McVitie knew he was in dead trouble, but he was a strong bugger and got away. He couldn't get through the door because one of the Lambrianous was in the way. So he ran across the room and tried to dive straight through a window. There was glass and broken wood everywhere. McVitie got his head and shoulders through, but the rest of him was stuck. He couldn't move, so we pulled him back by his legs.

By now he was crying. He wasn't the tough guy any more. Ron said to him, 'Be a man, Jack.'

McVitie said, 'I'll be a man but I won't fucking die like one.'

One of the others was holding McVitie's arms behind his back. I was handed a knife. It was a long one, a carving knife. I looked at McVitie and hated him for all the trouble he'd caused. I didn't think about it. I just pushed the knife into his face, near his eye. I just kept on stabbing him.

McVitie fell on the floor. Bender put his head to his chest and said he was dead. I felt relieved and a bit sick. I was glad it was over. There was blood everywhere, a lot of it on me. I felt I had to get out of the room.

We left the Lambrianous to clean up the place. Most of the others had already done a bunk. Ron and I went to a friend's in Hackney. We had a good scrub down and changed all our clothes. We left them there for our friend to burn. We got rid of the gun and the knife in the canal by Queensbridge Road.

They did me for the murder of Jack McVitie almost a year after the event, and they never found the body. They did my brother Charlie and Freddie Foreman for disposing of it – but that's ridiculous. People said McVitie had been buried in the foundations of a motorway or an office block. People said he'd been made into pig food or buried in Epping Forest or put in a furnace at a power station. People even said he'd been put in a coffin and cremated along with someone else. Only Ron and I know what really happened to the body, and we will probably take the secret to our graves. We will never incriminate the other people who were involved. We will never grass on them in the way that people have grassed on us to save their own skins. We would only reveal what happened to the body if we were both released and if everyone else involved was dead and could not be touched.

Despite everything it has cost me, I have never felt a moment's remorse. People from the Home Office used to come and see me at

Parkhurst. They always said, 'Don't you feel sorry you killed Jack McVitie?' If I had said, 'Yes I am very sorry, I never meant to do it,' it would probably have looked good on my reports. It might have even helped to get me out of gaol, or moved to a softer place than Parkhurst, or made my life in prison a bit easier. But I couldn't say it.

I *have* felt sadness for his family. Someone must have missed him, maybe even loved him. Well, for them I'm sorry.

I felt bad afterwards, though. I had a lot of nightmares. Not because I'd killed McVitie – one of the nastiest villains I have ever met – but because sticking a knife into anyone is not a pleasant thing to do. It would have been much easier and cleaner to have shot him. But killing isn't something you do lightly. *You* try to imagine what it's like to be in a dimly lit room, face to face with another man, and then stick a knife in him. Unless you're a psychopath – and I'm not – it's not an enjoyable feeling. It's a bloody awful feeling. And the panic afterwards, when you realize what you've done. What shall we do with the body? What am I going to do with the knife? What shall I do with my clothes? Will anyone grass on me? Maybe the coppers are on their way even now. And you try sleeping afterwards with so many thoughts going through your mind.

But soldiers have to kill the enemy, otherwise the enemy will kill them. No one calls soldiers murderers. And in a way we were soldiers, only our battleground was the streets of London.

I wouldn't kill now. I'm much older, much wiser, much more patient, and I've had a lot of time to think. But at the time it seemed the necessary thing to do.

Angelo Bruno was right, though: we shouldn't have done our own dirty work. I should have paid someone else to do it for me. Perhaps if McVitie had just been badly hurt it would have been different. But you can't turn the clock back. What's done is done and you have to pay the price. I think I've paid, all right – it's cost me nearly half my life.

Books and newspapers have said that I killed McVitie because I was under the influence of my brother, because I was frightened of him, because I was trying to prove that I was as tough as he was, because he had killed George Cornell. It's not true. I was not under Ron's influence. I am sick to death of people saying Ron was the bad one, the evil one, and I was the nice one, the weak one, who was led astray by him. I was every bit as bad – if bad is the word to use – as my brother. He didn't frighten me. Even in his black moods, when depressions hit him hard and the madness started to set in, I was never frightened of Ron. Why should I have been? Apart from Charlie and our mother, I was the one person in the world he would never have hurt, the one person he trusted in business matters. I never felt I had got to 'prove' myself to Ron by killing another man. He never tried to goad me into it.

McVitie was not the snivelling weakling that some books and articles have made him out to be. He was a tough customer, a man with the strongest arms I've ever seen, a man who was given to terrible violence. If I hadn't taken him out he would have got me – possibly killed me. Certainly he would have waited his chance and had me done over. So I killed him. And I'm not sorry, even though it's cost me so much. But I wouldn't kill again. The price was too high – even for the last supper of a man like Jack McVitie.

7

Ron: The Trial and the Traitors

'I am not going to waste words on you. In my view society has earned
a rest from your activities. I sentence you to life imprisonment,
which I recommend should not be less than thirty years.'

The words of Mr Justice Melford Stevenson, at the Old Bailey, on
8 March 1969. Just thirty-six words to condemn two men to a fate far
worse than death. Has Mr Melford Stevenson, with his silver-spoon,
public-school upbringing, ever realized his cruelty? What he did
to us was just as bad, worse, than anything we ever did to another
human being.

Can you imagine it? Put yourselves in our place for a few
moments. We were thirty-four years of age, in the prime of our lives.
We would not be free men again until we were sixty-four. The
chances of either of us being fit or sane by that time were slight. The
system, the authorities, were being allowed legally and systematic-
ally to destroy our bodies and our minds. And this in a so-called
civilized society.

Many would say we deserved it. Fair enough, they are entitled to
their opinion. But what about those who worked alongside us, whose
crimes were every bit as bad as ours? Was it really fair, was it really
justice, that they got away so lightly – and in some cases without any
penalty at all – in exchange for our liberty?

With very few exceptions the men we had supported and paid a
fortune all deserted us and gave evidence against us. And in their
vendetta against us the authorities forgave these men most of their
crimes in exchange for evidence which, in many cases, was a pack of
lies.

When Nipper Read and his army of policemen smashed their way
into my flat at Cedra Court at six o'clock in the morning on 9 May

1968, Reg and I gave up without a struggle. We'd only just gone to bed, very tired and fairly pissed after a night of pubbing and clubbing. The coppers handcuffed us both, though there was no need. They knocked my flat about a bit as they searched for weapons and drugs. They found neither, only an old crowbar I kept in the flat for my own protection.

We were taken by car, first to Scotland Yard – where we were officially arrested and cautioned – and then on to Brixton gaol, where we were to be held until the preliminary hearing at Old Street magistrates' court in July, when we and the police would discover if there was going to be a case for us to answer at a higher court.

When we got to Brixton we were taken to a special wing which had just been completed. It had electronic doors and all sorts of other security gadgets. We were the first people to use it. We were put in adjoining cells, but the screws had obviously been told to keep us apart. But even there we soon managed to find a couple of screws we could bribe, and soon information began coming in and out of Brixton.

One of the first messages we got was from Mad Frankie Fraser, who was downstairs in the prison itself. He'd been banged-up after the raid by the Richardson Gang on Mr Smith's Club in Catford. Frankie said he would give evidence for us in the Cornell case if we thought it would help. It was a nice gesture.

That was the start of our friendship with Frankie, who up to then we'd always regarded as our enemy. We later shared time at Broadmoor, and when he was eventually freed he used to come back to visit me. I was sorry when he got gaoled again on a robbery charge not too long ago. I'm afraid that another gaol sentence could well turn Frankie's mind altogether. I hope not, because he's a good bloke.

Other messages we were getting were not good. We began hearing stories that the law had arrested virtually every key member of the firm – Connie Whitehead, John Dickson, Chris and Anthony Lambrianou, Ron Bender and others. The word, also, was that several of them were cooperating with Nipper Read and his men in a bid to soften their own sentences. If this was true it was serious news. We couldn't believe it – we had looked after them all so well when they had worked for us.

95

Then the police pulled in our brother Charlie and Freddie Foreman. Foreman wasn't even on our firm, he operated his own businesses south of the river. Still free, at that time, we were told, were our cousin Ronnie Hart and Ian Barrie, my own right-hand man. We were confident we could trust both of them if they were caught.

Not long after, Hart was arrested hiding away in a caravan with a girl. And poor Ian Barrie, who was shattered by the collapse of the firm and the disappearance of virtually everybody he knew, was eventually cornered by the cops, pissed out of his head, in a pub in the East End. Ronnie Hart, sadly, collapsed under police pressure and talked. It was a wicked thing to do to your own cousins, and he knew it. Later he tried to commit suicide but – typically – he failed. After that he scarpered off to Australia, where he lives now.

As for Ian Barrie, he refused to say a word to the police. Ian was the best signing we ever made. He was spotted by one of our uncles, who thought he would make ideal material for the firm.

Barrie stayed loyal. So did Freddie Foreman and, of course, our brother Charlie. Virtually everyone else turned on us.

Life in Brixton gaol in those early days, in May and June 1968, wasn't bad. The screws treated us with respect and we were allowed quite a few privileges. Our mum used to bring our lunch in every day, usually cold chicken and salad and a bottle of wine. Several of our friends from the worlds of boxing and show business were allowed in to visit us as well. It was a funny feeling, rather like being in limbo. We knew we had a few problems, but we had such faith in ourselves and the fear we could put into people, we still believed we were going to get out of the mess. We still didn't believe, despite the rumours, that our mates, members of the firm, would go into the box and testify against us. That was the feeling in the East End too. Most people still believed the Krays would outfox the law once again. That's why people were still paying protection money to those of our collectors still outside – no one really believed we would go down for a long spell, and therefore no one wanted to face our wrath for non-payment of protection money once we got out again.

Nipper Read, Fred Gerrard and other cops came to see us and tried to question us, to put the frighteners on us – but we just told them all to fuck off.

Our preliminary trial, at Old Street magistrates court, began on 6 July 1968, in front of the Metropolitan Chief Magistrate, Frank Milton. We were taken to the court in a convoy of police vehicles, with motorcycle outriders. When we arrived we were amazed to find dozens of police and massive security. It was just like a Mafia trial in Italy. We hadn't seen any members of the firm who were supposed to be testifying against us. They and other witnesses were apparently in secret hideouts and the police were guarding them like hawks. No one could get near them. We knew that because we had tried to get messages to them, to ask them what the hell was going on, what the hell they thought they were doing. And also, to be honest, to warn them of the consequences of doing the dirty on us.

Normally the press are not allowed to report preliminary hearings, but we asked the magistrate to lift the ban. Reggie told him, 'We want the world to see the diabolical liberties the law has been taking.' The press, of course, were delighted because this was the biggest case they had covered for years.

We weren't sure what the police had got up their sleeves for this preliminary hearing, but we knew we might have a bit of bother when they produced Billy Exley to give evidence against us. Exley was really a nobody so far as we were concerned, certainly not a top man in the firm. He was an ex-boxer whom we'd used as muscle on a few occasions. Unfortunately, one occasion was to help guard Frank Mitchell, the Mad Axeman, after his escape from Dartmoor. Obviously, if Exley was going to reveal to the police that we *had* hidden Mitchell away, and if he was going to claim that we'd had Mitchell killed, then this was not a good start for us and was instrumental in our pleading guilty to harbouring him. The prosecution used Exley brilliantly. They told the magistrate that Exley had a bad heart, that it was possible he could die at any time and that he wanted 'to clear his conscience'.

Exley played his part well. His voice was soft, halting and uncertain. He didn't look too clever. He sat in a chair in the witness box and spoke into a microphone. The dying man purging his soul. The irony was that Billy's heart held out for another twenty years – he didn't die until late in 1987. We'd looked after Billy Exley well on the occasions he worked for us. In return he told the court what he knew about us, including plenty about the 'long firm' fraud, one of

97

the several phoney companies we'd formed in order to sell stock which didn't belong to us.

Exley had been the first target for Nipper Read and Fred Gerrard. He wasn't a big fish, but he was enough to set their ball rolling. And because of his poor health, he was an easy man for them to get at and break down. I could imagine them saying, 'Come on, Billy, we've got enough to put you inside. Your heart won't stand it, you know. You'll die in the nick. So what about it, eh? Just a few words on the Krays and you're a free man. We won't be troubling you again, Billy boy.' And, of course, Billy Exley fell for it. He knew what he'd done. He couldn't look us in the eye as he sat in the witness box.

As Exley staggered out Reg and I wondered what else the police had got up their sleeves. We've got to admit it, it was a masterstroke. Into court came the barmaid from the Blind Beggar pub, the one who'd been on duty the night I shot George Cornell. She looked as scared as a rabbit but, amazingly, Nipper Read had used one of his smooth-talking deputies (we later learned it was a copper called Mooney) to talk her into giving evidence. We knew straightaway that this was our first really big mistake. We knew at the time that the barmaid could identify both Ian Barrie and me as having been in the Blind Beggar that night. But we'd relied on that old East End wall of silence, that code of conduct which says you never grass to the law.

We had sent a message to the barmaid – via the manager of the Blind Beggar – to keep her mouth shut. But that's all we'd done. We hadn't been to see her personally, we hadn't made any threats to her or attempted any physical harm on her or her family, because that simply wasn't our style. It was a big mistake – we'd been too soft with a potentially key witness.

The moment the blonde barmaid began to give evidence against us a smile appeared on Nipper Read's face, a gleam of triumph. He knew he'd got us bang to rights.

I was crazy with anger. I realized how we'd been stitched up. Reggie and I were like two men trying to stop a dam breaking. And yet at the end of the day, if you really analyse it, we were done for by an ex-boxer with a dodgy ticker and a brainless barmaid who fell for a copper's charm. After that, it was going to be downhill all the way.

We were taken back to Brixton while plans were made for our full trial at the Old Bailey, which didn't in fact start until the following January. Those next five months, before our trial, were full of despair, frustration and anger. We couldn't get out, we couldn't get at the people who were destroying us, and the word came back, day after day, that our business empire was collapsing. Suddenly, for the first time, people thought we were going to go down – and for a long time. We knew it too, and as our trial approached we decided we would go down with dignity and style.

Even at the Old Bailey we were big box office. Tickets for the public gallery were selling at £5 a head on the black market – a lot of money in January 1969, especially for something which was supposed to be free.

There were many celebrities in the audience, including, on several days, the actor Charlton Heston. We had many letters and good-luck telegrams from people in show business, including one from Judy Garland. In fact I told the judge at one stage, 'If I wasn't here now I'd probably be having a drink with Judy Garland.' The press and the public loved that.

We behaved like gentlemen all the way through the trial, even though we had to listen to our former friends telling lies about us, and even though the judge, Melford Stevenson, tried to treat us like cattle. He wanted to make us wear numbers in court, so that we could be referred to as a number and not by our proper names. He was trying to strip away our last bit of dignity, our last bit of individuality. When they tried to put my number on me in the rooms below the court on the first day of the trial, I went wild. I told them I would kill them if they tried to put the number on me. I told them I would not go into the dock with a number on. And I sent a message to the judge on a slip of paper. It said simply: 'Get stuffed.' Melford Stevenson realized that he'd got a potential riot on his hands, so he backed down on the numbers idea and we were addressed by our proper names.

Only twice in court, during the thirty-nine days that the trial lasted, did we lose our cool. I lost my temper when the prosecuting counsel was describing how the police had confiscated our grand-parents' pension books. I called the prosecuting counsel a 'fat slob'. I don't regret that – I think it was fair comment.

Reggie got upset when they started talking in great detail about

99

the funeral of Frances and the circumstances of her death. He shouted out, 'The police are scum.'

We kept our dignity and our integrity. We could have named so many names in our trial – other villains, show business celebrities who'd done naughty things, even politicians and one or two churchmen. All these people were terrified we would name them – the media, of course, were hoping that we would – but we didn't. We never informed on anyone. We believe that two wrongs do not make a right. We believe we are better off than the rats who deserted our ship. They may have their freedom, but we have our self-respect. We still have our dignity – they have none.

We had two good men defending us, John Platts Mills QC and Paul Wrightson QC, both of whom became friends, but they faced an impossible task. The trial was wearing on both of us and every night we would be taken, shattered, back to our cells at Brixton. But every morning we would shave and shower, wash our hair, and put on our best blue suits and white shirts, and come back for more. The screws treated us OK, the police treated us OK, although they went completely over the top in their security arrangements. I suppose they were afraid attempts would be made to free us, but there was no one left who could have helped us escape.

Just three men remained loyal to us to the end and we shall be eternally grateful to them. Ian Barrie refused to say a word about us. He got twenty years for his part in the killing of George Cornell. Twenty years of hell in Durham gaol, yet he never complained once. Our brother Charlie got ten years for being an accessory to the murder of Jack McVitie, even though he was at home in bed at the time. They did him for helping to dispose of McVitie's body, even though McVitie's body was never found. But Charlie was a Kray, so he had to be put away. Then there was Freddie Foreman, who wasn't even a member of our firm. He was a close friend of Charlie's and they tied him in with Charlie on the disposal of McVitie's body. Freddie got ten years for that.

These were the men who stood by us. Not many, considering the small fortunes we'd paid out over the years to others and the way we'd looked after them and their families when they were inside. That was the hardest lesson of all for Reggie and me – that, for most people, loyalty is a dirty word.

100

Left: Diana Dors was a true friend, and so was her husband, Alan Lake. Here she is with mother, just after her book was published

Below: Alan and Diana with Charlie. *(Sunday People)*

Above: Reg's marriage to
Frances was the East
End wedding of the
year, and he was
shattered when she died.
But there were good
times in between

Left: On holiday in Italy

In the
clubs, like
'Freddie
Mills Nite
Spot'. . .

or just out
together.
(M. Escarcelle)

Reg's
flowers at
her funeral

Above: Lord Boothby — a friend and business associate of Ron

Left: Elaine, whom Ron married in Broadmoor, with her children. *(Anthony Steel)*

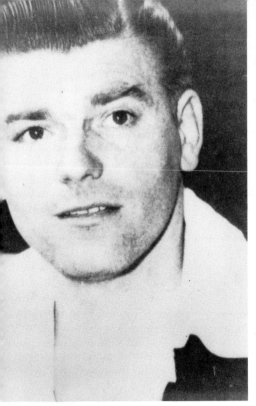

Frank Mitchell
known as the Mad Axeman

Anthony Lambrianou

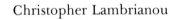

Christopher Lambrianou

and Fred Foreman

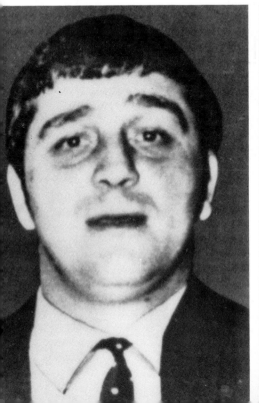

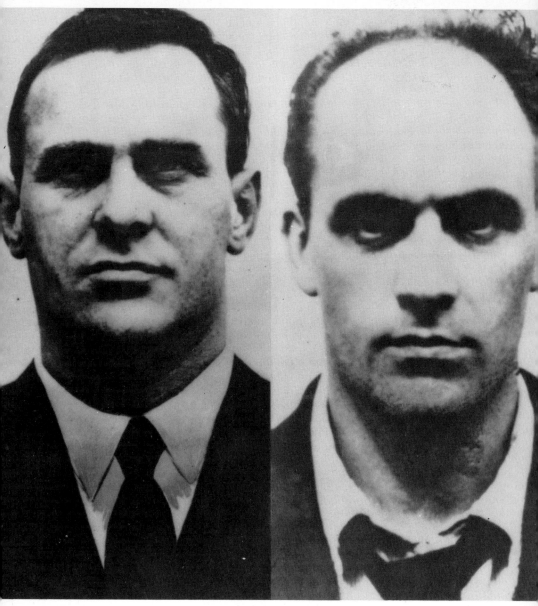

The two men who died: George Cornell and Jack 'the Hat' McVitie

Above left: A few more pictures from happier days. From Barbra Streisand to Ron

Above right: Us with Judy Garland and Mark Herron, her husband

Below: The two of us meet Joe Louis

Reg (left) and Ron arrive at their mother's funeral, August 1982 *(Syndication International* and *Rex Features)*

Reg, lifting weights at Parkhurst

We both appeared in the dock and we both denied everything. It made no difference. I went down for murdering George Cornell and being an accessory in the McVitie killing. Reg went down for murdering McVitie and being an accessory in the Cornell killing. The fact that he never knew it was going to happen, wasn't there and didn't hear about it until afterwards didn't seem to come into it!

The jury took six hours and fifty-four minutes to decide our guilt. The verdict was announced just after seven o'clock – at six minutes past seven, to be precise – on 8 March 1969. That was the moment the judge, Melford Stevenson, had been waiting for. The moment he would go down in history as the man who put the Kray twins away for thirty years apiece.

The way the Krays were treated pleased many people. But there were some who were concerned about this type of punishment. In the *Sunday Times* of 6 March 1969, Professor Leon Radzinwicz – Britain's leading authority at the time on long-term offenders – wrote: 'Society owes long-term prisoners something more than death in small doses.' And Lord Soper, the Methodist leader, said: 'Thirty years is more horrible than hanging. The procedure of putting them away and allowing them to rot is a more horrible fate than the quickness of the rope.' He added: 'Long-term prison sentences are an admission of failure. There has to be a ray of hope left for every man – whatever he has done.'

Lord Soper was right. He was right that allowing people to rot away is horrible. Both of us, I think – and we have never revealed this before – both of us, given the choice, would have preferred to hang. There has to be a ray of hope left.

The injustice of our sentences is easy to see. Dennis Nilsen killed sixteen young men – but he got a shorter sentence than us. George Stephenson burned five people to death in a house in the New Forest – but he got a shorter sentence than us. The Ealing rapists, Martin Macall and Christopher Byrne, got just ten years and eight years respectively. And the spy, Anthony Blunt – the biggest traitor of all – got precisely nothing. He wasn't even arrested. Yet how many lives was he responsible for?

The Prison Reform Trust's Una Padel was quoted recently as saying, 'It was the high emotion surrounding the Kray case that led to such a harsh sentence.'

I can still, as I sit here in my room in Broadmoor, recall our feelings after our trial was over and we were taken back to Brixton, before being shipped out to the prisons where we would begin our sentences. We were both shattered, absolutely shocked by what we had heard. We knew we would go down, knew we would get long sentences – but thirty years? We both managed to put on a brave, defiant face to the world. But once the screws had locked me up that night I don't mind admitting I broke down and cried. I couldn't see how I was going to get through the next thirty years. I said my prayers for the first time in a long time, I asked for Reg and me to be forgiven for the things we had done wrong. I couldn't face the thought of suicide, so I asked God if he would take my life, let me die, not put me through thirty years of hell. But, it's clear to me now, he couldn't have been listening.

8

The Women We Loved

Reg: On Frances

I've only ever loved – and I mean really loved – two women in my whole life. And I've lost them both. One was my mother and the other was my wife Frances. Ironically, it was Frances who died first. So I'll write about her first.

I met her in 1962 when Ron and I were really on the way to the top, to big success. We were already well known and well respected in the East End. I'd heard about Frances quite a bit, but I'd never actually met her. She was the sister of an old friend of mine called Frank Shea. One night I popped round to see Frank at the Shea family home in Ormsby Street, Bethnal Green. As chance, or fate, would have it, Frank wasn't there, but Frances was.

She opened the door and I found myself staring at the most beautiful girl I'd ever seen in my life. She had startling red hair and brown eyes, and the longest eyelashes I've ever seen, and a gentle, sweet smile. I was lost for words. For once in my life I didn't know what to say. I fell in love with her from the first moment I saw her. She was just eighteen years old.

We just stood there looking at each other. It felt like hours, although it was probably for no more than a few seconds. Finally, I said, 'Is Frank in?' I always was one for the quick, snappy line!

She said no, he wasn't there, but would I like to leave a message.

Suddenly I found myself blurting out, just like some teenage kid, 'Can I see you again? Can I take you out?'

She asked me where I wanted to take her.

I said, 'I don't know. Out for a ride in my car, anything.'

She nodded her head and said yes. And that was how it started – my love affair with Frances Shea.

I wasn't a kid. I was fully grown man. And I was getting used to

103

being in charge, with Ron, of some of the toughest characters in London town. Yet, in front of this slip of a girl, I was completely tongue tied!

Until then I had not had a lot of experience with girls. Sure, I'd been out with a few on one-night stands, but in those days, the early sixties, young girls weren't like they are now – they didn't open their legs to every Tom, Dick and Harry who came along. Nowadays, it seems to me what from I read in the papers and see on TV, you'd be lucky to find a virgin left in this country over the age of eighteen. But in those days it was different. Even if you were a fast-climbing young villain with money in your pockets, it still made no difference – nice girls still behaved in a decent fashion. Of course, even then you could always find scrubbers who would drop their pants at the flash of a fiver, but I've always hated cheap women and I've always hated the thought of catching something like VD. Now, of course, because moral standards are so low, everyone seems in danger of dying from Aids.

No, Frances was very much an old-fashioned, decent sort of girl, and that was the way I liked it. Contrary to popular belief, our mum had brought Ron and me up with a strong sense of moral values. Ron couldn't help the fact that the way his body was made meant that he would be more attracted to young men than young women. It wasn't his fault. But even so he was never promiscuous. He always had one friend at a time and would stick with that person. He never put it about all over the place like they do nowadays. We had certain standards. And although I had been out with a few girls casually and knew what sex was all about, I knew straightaway that Frances was going to be different.

This wasn't going to be a one-night stand or just a few casual dates. Not as far as I was concerned. This was something more serious. I've never known anything like it. From the moment I met Frances I couldn't concentrate on my work, nothing seemed important any more except being with her. If you've ever been in love you will know what I mean.

On our first date I took her to the Double R Club, which we owned. Normally, I would sit with the customers and chat and drink. But on this particular night, the night of our first date, we just sat there and listened to the juke box. We had only two drinks all evening. We were totally oblivious to everyone else. It was beautiful. I remember she said to me, 'Some time ago I came by this club with my girlfriends and we peeked in through the door. Then a man came out and we all ran away.'

That summed her up really. She was just a kid. She was eighteen, but a very young and pure and innocent eighteen. She had the body of a woman, but the sweet mind of a child. In many ways she *was* still a child and I treated her like a little princess. I suppose in some ways I must have seemed quite old to her.

I would see Frances nearly every night, then, after I had dropped her off back at her house, I would go on to work in the clubs or on a tour round our spielers, whatever needed doing that particular night.

We used to go to pubs and have a gin and tonic together. I would give the barman a ten pound note and then, with the change he had given me, Frances and I would play a game. I would ask her for the East End slang names for each of the coins. For example, a half-crown (2s 6d) was a 'tosheroon', 5s was a 'caser', a ten shilling note – half a quid – was a 'cow's calf', a five pound note was a 'jack', and so on. There were many more names. Every time Frances remembered the name correctly I'd chuck the money in her handbag. Sometimes she would win up to £25 a night. It was a simple little game but we'd play it often and she really enjoyed it.

She brought a wonderful sort of simplicity into my life. But she wasn't simple. In fact, when I got to know her, I realized she was a deep person, a complex girl. And this is another side of her character that writers have never revealed. For example, we used to talk a lot about the future. We would sit in my car, late at night, and on more than one occasion she said to me, 'I don't think I will ever be old – I know I will never reach old age.' She had this feeling, this premonition, that she would die soon after she was twenty-one. She would get quite distraught when she talked about it. I used to try to pacify her, tell her that it wouldn't happen, that she wouldn't die young. As it happened, I was wrong – Frances died when she was twenty-three, in the most awful and tragic circumstances.

Sometimes, in my car, she would stare at the stars shining above the streets of the East End, and she would say, 'I know if I get to Heaven there will be a big black horse up there, waiting for me.' She was crazy about horses – perhaps due to her Irish ancestry.

105

Once I bought her an imitation gold ring from a market trader called Red Face Tommy. It was just a simple little gift – but you would have thought I had bought her the Crown Jewels. She really treasured that ring and couldn't bear to take it off her finger. It only cost a few quid, but to her it was priceless. It became a sort of engagement ring.

But Frances's mind, I believe, was put into a state of turmoil by her parents. She was so lovely, so innocent, that they couldn't bear the thought of losing her, of letting her go. I can understand that, but what I couldn't understand was their hostility towards me. I would never have taken their daughter away from them completely. I would always have shared her. She could have spent as much time as she wanted with them and I would never have objected. I wanted to be part of a big secure family. But they didn't like me and they didn't like the thought of Frances leaving home and getting married. So they did everything they possibly could to break us up. They put her in a very difficult and confusing position – she was in love with me and yet she also had love and respect for them. She didn't know what to do to make everyone happy. She was so happy with me and we'd have lovely evenings together, then she'd go home and her parents would go on at her for going out with a gangster.

These days, of course, Frances would simply have left home and moved in with me. But it wasn't like that then. We are talking about a time when kids, especially young girls, had to show respect to their parents.

I was never welcome at their house, almost from the word go. But Frances was always welcomed at Vallance Road. My mother loved her and once Frances said to me, 'I get on better with your mum than I do with my own mum.'

I suppose her parents weren't happy because of the kind of work I did and the sort of people I mixed with – but I always tried to keep Frances away from that side of things. It's true I took Frances to several functions at our clubs when we had stars appearing there, but she enjoyed going to things like that. In any case, her dad worked in one of our clubs for a time – he was happy to take our money, it seems, but not happy for his daughter to mix with the bloke who was making it.

The problems really began to get worse when I took her away on

106

holiday to Milan – just the two of us. That was in 1963. We had a great time in that beautiful city. We went to La Scala to see *Madame Butterfly*. It was wonderful and when we got back to London we went to the Green Gate pub, in Bethnal Green Road, with its rowdy music, to compare it with the music we had heard in Italy. The comparison was interesting, to say the least.

Frances and I loved to travel. Later we went to Barcelona. We saw a bullfight, which we hated. We went to Catalonia Square, in the middle of Barcelona, with its amazing water fountains, and we sat there for several hours, eating apples, drinking coke, and just watching. We were happy and it was great.

When we got back from those trips she'd get a lot of stick from her parents. I once went round to try to make peace and asked Mr and Mrs Shea if I could marry Frances. It wasn't the first time I had asked, and it wasn't the first time they had said no. On this occasion Frances burst into tears and I left the house angrily, slamming the door behind me.

Then I got sent to Wandsworth for six months after being found guilty of demanding money with menaces (the business with Daniel Shay, which is mentioned in chapter 2). It was a terrible time. I was on the inside and the girl I loved was on the outside. I was convinced I would lose her, that her parents would talk her round to their point of view, and that she would find someone else to love. But then she wrote to me. Her letter said: 'I am sorry you are in prison. Don't worry. When you come out I'll make your favourite toast and marmalade for your breakfast. I love you. Please remember me.' Please remember! How could I forget her? I couldn't get her out of my mind.

But it was the Wandsworth business, I believe, that was the final straw as far as Frances's parents were concerned. They could see that she was in love with me and so they tried harder than ever to split us up. But I, being the mug I am, still employed her father – Frank – in one of our clubs.

Then, in 1965, Ron, and I were up at the Old Bailey, charged with demanding money with menaces – protection money – from a Soho club owner (Hew McCowan, see chapter 2) – and it seemed that the strains were going to be too much for our relationship. But the judge told the jury that if they didn't think McCowan was a reliable witness, they should not find us guilty, and we were acquitted. It had taken a long time, but we were free men. Frances was waiting for me when I came out and at the celebration party afterwards I proposed again and she said yes – with or without her parents' permission. Under that sort of pressure they virtually had to give in, and they did.

We were married on 19 April – Primrose Day – in 1965 at St James the Great Church in Bethnal Green. Frances was twenty-one. She looked bloody ravishing. She wore a full-length white dress, her lovely red hair was pulled back. It was the East End's 'marriage of the year'. Ron was my best man and among the two hundred guests were boxers Terry Allen, Terry Spinks and Ted 'Kid' Lewis, the Clark Brothers, and several other big stars of the time. David Bailey took the wedding photographs and we drove to the reception at the Finsbury Park Hotel in a maroon Rolls-Royce. We received dozens of telegrams, including one from Judy Garland, Billy Daniels, Barbara Windsor, Lita Roza and Lord Boothby. It was an incredible day. After that we went on honeymoon to Athens. That honeymoon was one of the happiest times of my life, but some vicious lies have been written about it. It was claimed, for instance, that I couldn't make love. I could name one or two women to whom I *had* made love before I met Frances. They would have proved that I am as good a lover as the next man. But I'm not that much of a lout that I would expect any woman to stand up and admit, 'I made love to Reggie Kray.'

Ironically, at about the same time as all these allegations, a twenty-nine-year-old waitress by the name of Ann Zambodini, from Poplar, took me to court claiming I was the father of her daughter. The magistrate dismissed the case through lack of evidence – or, to quote him, 'lack of corroboration of her evidence'. The magistrate was right. But clearly Miss Zambodini didn't think I was impotent.

It's a funny old world, isn't it? A family saying you haven't made love to their daughter, and you know you have, and a woman saying that you've made love to her and given her a kid, and you know you haven't. Talk about a no-win situation!

It was later claimed by one newspaper that I'd got drunk on the first night of the honeymoon and locked Frances in our bedroom. Then I subsequently got drunk on every night of the honeymoon.

Again, lies. The fact is, Frances and I had a perfectly normal honeymoon and a normal relationship after it.

When we got home from the honeymoon the problems started again. We went to live with Mr and Mrs Shea for a few weeks while our own flat was being decorated. I had to go back to work, and that meant going out late at night to our various business enterprises. Then Frances wanted to return to her job as a secretary, but I didn't want her to. It didn't seem right that Reggie Kray's wife should be working. I wanted her to live in the grand style, I wanted her to be a lady of leisure. This was a mistake on my part. Looking back, I was being a bit selfish. I should have let her go back to work – she would have been much happier working.

We still had some good times though. I remember some very happy evenings at the Blue Angel, a very exclusive club off Berkeley Square. Noel Harrison was in cabaret there and Frances was a very big fan of his. We saw him several times and he would always come over to our table for a chat. He seemed a very nice bloke.

But gradually the unsociable hours that I worked, plus the fact that Frances was cooped up all day, meant that cracks began to appear in our marriage. The strain of several years began to tell. Eventually, after a few months, Frances left me and went back home. It wasn't a violent parting – we just agreed to separate for a while until we could sort things out.

I kept going round to the Sheas' house to see her, but her parents wouldn't let me in. I would find myself standing in the street talking to my own wife, with her standing by the bedroom window. I would go round during the day with money for her, but her parents would say she wasn't in. My in-laws took the money and I'd tell them to make sure that Frances got it.

By now she was in a state of complete mental torment. She disappeared from home. Her mother told me she was staying with a friend 'out of town'. In fact she was in Hackney hospital, suffering from acute depression. She was really ill. I finally found out where she was and went to see her. She was doped up to the eyeballs.

And that's another thing I want to make very clear – I never, ever got Frances on drugs. I hate drugs – I always have. After Frances came out of hospital our relationship began again, but she simply wasn't the same bright, vivacious girl I'd known before. The drugs and the mental strain were destroying her. So was her conviction that she was going to die soon. She became almost impossible to calm down. But I refused to give her drugs, so she left me again and returned home, where she knew she could have them. Then she was hospitalized again, this time in a nursing home in Camden Town. I kept going to see her and was alarmed at the way she was going downhill.

On 7 June 1967 I awoke, alone, with the most awful premonition. I had dreamed that Frances was dead. I was sweating with fear. I rushed round to her parents' home and was told by a neighbour that Frances was dead. She had died, from an overdose of drugs, at her brother's house, in Wimbourne Street, Hoxton. I could not believe it. My beautiful Frances dead.

The next days were a bloody nightmare. Frances was buried at Chingford, in Essex. It was an awful, terrible, painful day. For her funeral I had a card printed with her photograph and a poem I had written. It is called 'If'.

> If I could climb upon a passing cloud
> That would drift your way,
> I would not ask for a more beautiful day.
> Perhaps I would pass a rainbow,
> with nature's clouds so beautifully aglow,
> If you were there at journey's end
> I would know,
> It was the beginning – and not the end.

I meant every word. And yet, in my moment of grief, one national newspaper actually said that my poem and the many flowers that I sent to my own wife's funeral were an act of 'ostentation'. Believe me, when you are down they will kick you until you stay down. All that kept me going through those days was the memory of Frances saying, 'If I go to Heaven there'll be a big black horse up there waiting for me.'

The days, the weeks, the months after Frances died were, for me, a nightmare seen through a sort of alcoholic haze. Gin was the only way for me to blot out all that had happened.

I will never forget my little Frances. I loved her and she loved me.

I had lost one of the two women I had loved in my life. The other was my mother, who was a great support to me at this time. She knew the agony I went through, the torture.

I still think about it all so often. I would dearly like, before I die, to make my peace with Frances's parents, but so many harsh things were said that I believe it will not be possible.

With Frances gone, my life was never going to be the same again. Part of me died when she died and I stopped caring about things. The rest of me died when my mother passed away.

After all that pain, everything the Home Office and the prison authorities throw at me now will not smash me – there is nothing left to smash.

Ron: On Our Mother

I believe – and the others may hate me for saying this – but I believe it was Reg, Charlie and I who finally killed our mother. Twice a week for fourteen years she would visit Reg and me (and Charlie when he was inside), and in the end it was all too much for her. She would never admit it – she always came to see us even when she wasn't well, and we told her not to. When we first went down, Reg was at Parkhurst and I was at Durham. So you can imagine the hundreds of miles our mother travelled every week. Yet, despite all the heart-aches we gave her, she was a tower of strength.

I had a terrible time at Durham. I missed Reggie dreadfully and I had serious mental problems, but the prison officers there were very unsympathetic. I was a real target for them and they made my life hell. Early on, I went on hunger strike in protest at the way I was being treated. I went without food for fourteen days. Another time I got fifty-six days' solitary confinement for thumping a guard who was provoking me. The screws were always taking the piss, trying to wind me up, so I slung a pot of urine over one of them. The other guards kicked me all along the landing, but a kind old screw by the name of Chief Bunker stopped them, saying, 'Leave him alone. He's had enough.' Since then I've always sent Chief Bunker a card every Christmas.

My mother could see the terrible things that were happening and she could see that being away from Reg was making my problems worse. So she campaigned endlessly to get me and Reg reunited. She wrote to the papers and to the Prime Minister and finally, because of her efforts, I was moved to Parkhurst.

That was in 1972 and my move cut down her travelling quite a bit, but it was still hard on her. All the way down to Southampton, then the ferry to the Isle of Wight, and the prison bus to Parkhurst, But she always kept coming. When I got transferred to Broadmoor, she would come to see me once a week, and Reg once a week, even when her health began to go downhill.

She was the best mum three lads ever had and I'm crying now as I think about her. I wish that we hadn't given her so many problems. She never deserved it. She was such a good woman – the best.

She died in August 1982. That was a time of despair. The best thing, the best person, in our lives, was gone.

Mum was cremated at Romford crematorium in Essex. It was the saddest day of my life, and what made it even sadder was the fact that the police and the press turned it into a bloody carnival. The authorities did the right thing by me and Reg. They recognized the bond between us and our mum, so they agreed that we could go to her funeral. And they looked after us when we got there, with lunch and a cup of tea at Romford police station. But when we arrived at the crematorium, it was bloody chaos. There were hundreds of people there with dozens of pressmen and television people. It wasn't fair. It wasn't right. It should have been a private occasion.

The crowd nearly caused a riot when Reg and I arrived. We were handcuffed to the two biggest officers they could find in the prison service. Reg was angry, saying they did that on purpose to try to make us look like two dwarves. There were police helicopters flying around in the sky and the church was even searched for bombs. They went completely over the top on what should have been a solemn, simple, silent service.

Among the congregation at the funeral service was Billy Hill. Both Reg and I wanted to shake him by the hand, probably for the last time, as he was then over seventy years old, but it wasn't possible. Later Billy wrote to me and said, 'If I could share some of your sentence, I would be willing. I doubt if we will ever meet again but always remember that my heart will be with you in spirit.'

Joe Louis, the former heavyweight champion of the world, also wrote to us saying how sorry he was.

Reg and I did not say a lot to each other at the funeral. After all, what was there to say? We had lost our mother, the woman who had meant the world to us, the lady who had brought us up well against all the odds, who had given us so much love and kindness. I felt I'd lost everything. My Auntie Rose had gone years before, now my mum. Poor Reg had also lost Frances.

Our old dad was at the funeral, but he'd had the stuffing knocked out of him by then and died a year later. We weren't allowed out for his funeral, but we'd never been as close to him as we'd been to our mum. In any case, he'd asked for a quiet funeral – especially after what he'd seen at our mother's funeral.

When the service was over and all the people had gone away, Reg got into his prison van to be driven back to Parkhurst and I got into the van that was to take me back to Broadmoor. I have not been out again since. And I thought about a poem I had written about our mum. I called it 'To a Beautiful Mother'.

> When I look at the silver
> In your hair.
> How I wish you never in the world
> Had a care.
> How I wish week after week
> It was not always, Hello and Goodbye,
> You have made the weeks, months,
> And years fly by.
> You have been our rainbow
> In a dark sky.
> We hope that one day it will be
> Just, Hello.
> And never again goodbye.

9

Reg: Life in Parkhurst

Life in Parkhurst was a living hell. It was like living in a jungle – a constant battle for sanity and survival. You never knew what horrors, unpleasantness and indignities the next day would bring. In my time there I had met and mixed with many of the notorious criminals this country has produced in the past couple of decades, and a good many from overseas as well. The cop killers Harry Roberts, John Duddy and Christopher Craig, the moors murderer Ian Brady, the spy Peter Kroger, the Great Train Robbers – I've seen them all. I've shared my time with murderers, terrorists, rapists and thieves.

It's because of my own attitude to prison life, because of my mental approach to my problems, because of my friends, my hobbies and my fanaticism for physical fitness that I have not been sent insane. I believe that that is what the prison authorities wanted, and what they still want – to send me mad so that they can lock me away in a madhouse for ever. I promise them, no matter how long they keep me, no matter what they do to me, *they will never succeed*.

I was kept as a Category A prisoner for seventeen years – far longer than was necessary. I wasn't a danger to anyone else. And I wasn't an escape risk – in all my years at Parkhurst I never once attempted to escape. Finally, in a desperate attempt to get taken off Category A I sent a proverb to the Home Secretary:

> One will never learn to swim
> Unless one goes into the water.
> And I will not be able to adapt again to society,
> Unless given a chance to do so.

It helped to get me off Category A, even if it didn't get me any closer to full or even part parole.

Parkhurst itself is an ugly, grey building near Newport in the centre of the Isle of Wight. Isle of Wight? It should be called Isle of Prisons because it's also the home of Albany prison, where a lot of the IRA terrorists are kept, and Camp Hill prison, where Ron once spent some time. I've seen holiday brochures advertising the beauty of the Isle of Wight. Maybe I'm biased but, as one of its longest-serving residents, I wouldn't go back there if it was the last fucking place on earth that hadn't been bombed by the Russians.

Inside, Parkhurst is like something out of a Dickens novel, with its wooden floorboards, lumpy porridge and a single greasy sausage for breakfast. We get so used to the poor-quality food that no one really grumbles. How does one piece of toast with a layer of cheese, a layer of beans and an egg on top sound for Sunday lunch? That's the kind of thing we get most weeks. Or we might get a slice of beef cut so thin, a couple of mouthfuls and it's gone.

A cell is always a depressing place, especially at Parkhurst, where the floorboards are painted blue, and a very faded, chipped blue at that. So much of Parkhurst is made of wood that if an arsonist were to ply his trade, everyone would be fried alive in a matter of minutes. I'm surprised that it's never happened.

My cell at Parkhurst consisted of one cupboard with six small compartments – the whole thing less than a yard square – in which to keep my clothes, a table and chair, and, of course, a bed. I was allowed to have two pairs of pants, two pairs of socks, two shirts, one jumper and a pair of shoes. I also had a sweatshirt and trainers.

You can either have a record player or a cassette player, plus a radio. The radio is very important to me – I don't think I've missed 'Friday Night Is Music Night' once in the past twenty years.

We lived our lives by rules and regulations, regulations like the following, which are issued to every prisoner:

Items of property which may be handed or sent in by prisoners'
relatives and friends

The following is the complete list of items prisoners may have handed or sent in to them. Other items will not normally be accepted and, if posted in, prisoners will not be allowed them in possession.

115

Cell Furnishings:
1. Bedspread – single size only.
2. Curtains – no curtain wire or fixings allowed.
3. Floor mat – up to 6 ft × 3 ft.
4. Table Cover.

Toiletries:
Battery Shaver.

Hobbies:
Budgerigars – 1 only and bird cages can be handed in.

General items:
1. Books – hardbacks or paperbacks in good condition. Only 12 allowed in possession. No library books allowed.
2. Cassette Player – this may be allowed instead of a record player. It must be battery operated, not be fitted with a recording facility (altered sets not allowed) and have no carrying case. *PLEASE NOTE:–* Cassette tapes may *not* be handed in. Only commercially pre-recorded cassettes are allowed which must be supplied direct from established British retail suppliers or registered clubs. No home recordings or family messages allowed.
3. Calendar – no padded calendars are allowed.
4. Crucifix.
5. Ear-piece for radio.
6. Greetings Cards – these may not be padded. Only completed written cards allowed – no blanks.
7. Headphones.
8. Medallion.
9. Musical instruments – harmonica, woodwind or small string instrument, only one instrument allowed.
10. Newspapers and Magazines – these must come direct from a registered newsagent.
11. Photographs and Pictures – unglassed pictures only allowed and posters must not exceed 4 ft × 3 ft.
12. Prayer Mat and Prayer Caps – only allowed if they are needed for the practice of a prisoners' registered religion.

13. Radio – must not receive VHF or FM and must be battery powered. Altered and decorated sets are not allowed.
14. Record Player and Accessories – this is an alternative to a cassette player and must be battery operated only. It may have up to 2 speakers.
15. Records – a maximum of 25 LPs or EPs allowed in possession. Records are only allowed for prisoners with record players.
16. Rosary Beads.
17. Smoking Requisites – up to 3 pipes, one tobacco pouch and a tinder lighter are allowed. Prisoners may also have up to 4 packets of pipe cleaners.
18. Vacuum Flask – this must have a plastic outer casing and a maximum capacity of 2 pints.
19. Ring – a plain band wedding ring or signet ring may be allowed. Other wedding rings, including those containing stones, will be considered on application.
20. Wrist-watch – wrist-watches with alarm facilities are allowed. Not stopwatch facilities.
21. Calculators. Programmable or printout tapes not allowed.
22. Bird cages. One only either metal or wood. Maximum size 28″ × 18″ × 16″.

NB: No batteries may be handed or sent in.

Our lives were governed by routine. The day always began at 8 o'clock – unlock for breakfast, morning shaves, showers, etc. Work was from 9 a.m. to 10.45. The work was menial, but kept the mind occupied. It varied from cleaning landings, working in the kitchens, to tailoring and sheet metal work. Nothing much was learned or gained from these jobs, but the British prison system is not designed for rehabilitation – retribution is the name of the game. After labour we had exercise for an hour, when we could go for a walk or run around the exercise yard. In Parkhurst that's quite a large area. Then it's bang up for lunch until 1.40 p.m., then unlock and maybe a quick shower. Afternoons were labour again from 1.55 to 4.15; 5 p.m. bang up for tea; 6 p.m. unlock for evening association, which is when the cons can either watch TV, play table tennis, sit around and chat or go to the gym for a one-hour session. That's what I normally did. We banged up again at 9 p.m. for the night and either listened to the radio or records, wrote letters or just sat and thought until sleep eventually came, if it came at all.

The basic prison wage is about £2.50, out of which the prisoners can buy extra food, chocolate or tobacco. I spend practically all my pay on writing letters. Apart from the gym, writing is my only outlet for my frustrations. I honestly have no vices.

I get letters from all over the country, often from people I've never met or heard of. For instance, as I'm writing this, alongside me is a letter I received today from a prisoner at Lewes prison. I won't name him, but I'll quote from his letter.

> I hope you don't mind a letter from someone you have heard nothing about. I may have been mentioned, just in conversation, by an ex-inmate called John Masterson, with whom I shared a cell in the Scrubs.
>
> I'm a great admirer of yours. I think you are in a class on your own. I am also an old Hoxton boy, but decided to move away from it all.
>
> As you may know, it's not the same place any more. I really don't know what to say to you at the moment, but if you wouldn't mind, I'd like to write to you now and then.
>
> If there is anything you need, you are more than welcome.
>
> All the best, Reg . . .

I get many letters like that from cons in other prisons. I'm something of a folk hero to the younger cons.

Night-time is the worst time for most prisoners. Sometimes, in the quiet of the night, when everyone was locked up, I would theorize about the men in the cells next door to mine, locked up with their dreams and emotions in this human zoo.

Some nights I have really bad dreams. Usually it is the same nightmare. I'm trapped in a small yard or tunnel and can't get out. I get claustrophobic. I'm trying to climb over huge piles of dead fish. I'm trying and trying, to no avail. It just goes on and on until I wake up sweating and more tired than when I went to sleep. I used to have similar dreams when I was a kid. It's as if I was always destined to be incarcerated, with no light at the end of the tunnel.

On the nights when this happens to me I take off my sweatshirt and strip to the waist, and walk around my cell. Round and round like a bloody caged animal. I've taught myself to keep calm.

Parkhurst is a little community, and like most others it's run on its own rules and understandings. There are all sorts there: Indians, Pakistanis, French, Jews, Germans, Turks, Italians, Brazilians, Greeks, Moslems, Mormons, Catholics, etc., all under one roof. As if that wasn't a recipe enough for problems, there's every sort of prisoner there, from simple robbers to IRA terrorists. We were forced to get along and could only do so if we followed a rigid code of conduct.

Grasses or informers were not tolerated. If caught, they were attacked. Child molesters and granny bashers were also treated the same way – we made their lives hell. They usually finished up on Rule 43, which means they were constantly under the protection of the prison officers. However, an officer could often be bribed to be 'distracted' for the thirty seconds or so it took to punish a con who needed correction.

There were many different firms in a prison like Parkhurst, and before any trouble started one firm always tried to learn the strengths and weaknesses of a rival firm, and also which firms could be relied upon to affiliate in times of trouble and unrest. This politicking is often what stops trouble or solves a problem before it gets off the ground. You always have to consider your enemy's allies before taking any form of action. Sometimes, of course, the whole thing can work in reverse, and the fact that some firms will back up others means that a small problem can end up in a war involving half the prison.

Frustration is a common cause of trouble, and violence is often the only solution to a problem. I think it was the introduction of terrorists into British prisons that led to an increase in tension and violence. Ordinary British prisoners tend to hate these foreign bastards who've caused so much unhappiness and so many problems for our people. They were the cause of some horrendous battles in Parkhurst, battles which rarely got the attention of the media.

I remember one night, shortly before I left Parkhurst, in January 1987, one of a group of Israeli prisoners was cut on the face early in the evening. It was his own fault – he'd made an anti-British remark which didn't go down too well with one of the English lads. The cutting of the Israeli led to a full-scale confrontation between several

119

Israeli prisoners and some of their foreign friends and a large gang of British cons. There was some nasty scuffling and scrapping on the landing above mine. It was obvious that weapons were being used and Pete Gillett, a close friend of mine, wanted to get involved when he saw one of our mates getting into a bit of bother. He started to climb the stairs to the landing above, but I pulled him back by a chain that he wore round his neck. I pulled him so hard I broke the chain. He was not best pleased, but realized later that I'd done him a big favour. Several cons – both Israeli and English – got very badly cut about in the scrap, and early the next morning fourteen prisoners were shifted to other prisons as a result of the trouble, even though some were only trying to stop the fighting.

I've seen this sort of thing many times over the years. In fact, when I was younger and wilder I would always get involved. Hit first and ask questions later. But as the years go by, and you've had a few private beatings by the screws when you've done something wrong, you learn your lesson and keep out of trouble whenever possible. In prison you can't win if you step out of line – if other cons don't get you the screws will, or you end up spending time in the punishment block.

After the fight I've just mentioned they strip-searched and then used a new metal-detecting bodyscanner on all the cons involved. It's amazing just how many weapons, some of them really deadly knives, are smuggled into prisons like Parkhurst. The officers are supposed to search all visitors before they come in, but, like drugs, weapons are an accepted part of everyday life at Parkhurst.

I didn't live by violence in Parkhurst, though I let it be known that anyone who picked on me would get it back, and get it back bloody hard. Some cons, though, when they come inside, try to live their lives as they did outside. For instance, Charlie Mitchell, a con I had known for many years, died as he had lived – violently. He was murdered by another con who couldn't take any more of his bullying ways. In days gone by Charlie had done some work for our firm. He went with our accountant, Les Payne, and our brother Charlie to Montreal to talk business with the Canadian Mafia. The three of them were hauled off the plane at Montreal airport after the Canadian authorities had had a tip-off they were arriving. Their passports were confiscated, they were bunged in a local prison and eventually slung out of Canada as 'undesirables'. Some might say, 'Fair comment!'

Charlie Mitchell died in a moment of madness and one man who won't miss him will be Danny La Rue. Some years ago Charlie hit Danny on the jaw at Winston's Club in London, where Danny used to sing. Quite what sparked Charlie into one his rages, I don't know, but it's said Danny still has a scar on his jaw. Ron and I decided eventually that Mitchell was a luxury even we couldn't afford – he was actually far more violent than we were!

I mentioned Harry Roberts, the cop killer, at the start of this chapter. Funnily enough, he's now with me again, at Gartree prison, in Leicestershire. Hate 'Em All Harry they used to call him, and I believe he killed three coppers without a moment's hesitation or remorse. Yet I saw him scream and nearly faint one day at Parkhurst when he cut his finger on a knife he was using to cut up his meat. When I asked him what the matter was he told me he couldn't stand the sight of blood.

Another killer was Bonnie Paul, who killed his own brother, Andy, who used to work on the door of several of our clubs. Andy was a smashing bloke but he had a disagreement with Bonnie, who blasted him in the stomach with a shotgun. As he lay on his deathbed, breathing his last, a police sergeant leaned over his bed and whispered in his ear, 'Quick, give me the name of the man who killed you.'

Andy looked at him, smiled sweetly, and said, 'Fuck off!' Then he died.

Christopher Craig was in Parkhurst in my early days. He was inside for killing a copper with a mate of his called Bentley, who was hanged. Craig used to walk about staring at the ground, his hands stuffed deep in his pockets. In those days of hanging, he was a lifer. Then, lifers were regarded as a novelty, a curiosity. Now they are ten a penny.

I never got to know Craig – he was a sad, lonely, isolated figure. You tend to stick with your own kind in prison and Craig wasn't really like us, he wasn't a professional. He was an amateur who'd bungled it and, as far as he was concerned, it had proved a costly mistake.

Mind you, even some of our own kind could make me sick with

their perverted ways. Dennis Stafford was a classic example. He used to show other cons photos of his victim on the morgue slab, with two bullet holes quite visible. God knows where he got them from, but he would hand them around as others might show wedding photographs. When he tried to show them to me once, I told him fairly clearly where he could stick them. That sort of thing isn't my scene.

I have known of several other cases of gruesome photos being shown around. The so-called Cambridge Rapist used to show pornographic-type photos of his victims to other cons in exchange for half-ounce tins of tobacco.

You meet all sorts inside. There was another con who used to swallow bed springs. He had three operations on his stomach to get rid of them all. After he'd swallowed a few of his bed springs, I told him that he ought to try sit-ups to strengthen his stomach. A bit sick, I know, but if you didn't laugh sometimes in prison you'd definitely finish up crying. I tell you, it's a mad, mad world in here.

I met Peter Kroger, the spy, too. I was not that keen on him, even though after he was released he sent me a card from Poland. Traitors aren't my favourite people, they do so much damage. Yet they always seem to get away fairly lightly. It bloody amazes me that someone like Kroger has actually damaged the whole country, yet walks away a free man – admittedly in another country – but Ron and I, who only damaged other villains, are still banged up.

I also hate sex offenders and people who hurt old people. I don't even like most cop killers, though Harry Roberts is an exception. Towards the end of my stay at Parkhurst we had several cop killers there: Harry Roberts, Bill Skingle, who is doing natural life for shooting a policeman nine times, Fred Searle and – until he died of a stroke – John Duddy. We also had Stuart Blackstock, the guy who shot PC Olds.

Many of the so-called Great Train Robbers have passed through Parkhurst as well – but Ron and I were never particularly impressed with what they did, all except Ronnie Biggs, who's given the law more than a run for their money.

I've even met the second wife of Jack McVitie there – visiting her present husband, who was serving fourteen years. I had met her outside a few times, so we would meet and talk to each other, and I was also on friendly terms with her new husband. As I've said before, all of *our* business was business – it was never personal, and that's why we can remain on good terms with people like McVitie's ex-wife and the Richardson brothers and Mad Frankie Fraser, even though, at one time, we might have been deadly enemies.

We have our own code of conduct and live by it – that's what the authorities don't seem to realize. Part of my philosophy, for example, has taught me never to think about those who gave evidence against me in their role of Judas, because then I would be a bitter man, a loser. As it is, because I don't ever think about them, I am a winner.

I was guilty of one moment of weakness in Parkhurst, though. Some years ago I tried to commit suicide. It had nothing to do with the length of my sentence, though that, naturally, has often depressed me. No, I became the victim of paranoia. I began to believe that my family would be in danger if I remained alive. Someone – I was convinced – wanted me out of the way, dead. And that someone – that person in my mind – would kill my family if he couldn't kill me, because he knew that if he killed my family he would, in effect, kill me at the same time. That would be his revenge.

I became convinced that the only way to save my family – my mother and father and brothers – was to kill myself, to take my own life. That way the person who was after me would be satisfied. So one night I smoked what I thought would be a last cigarette, said my prayers and broke the glass from the spectacles I used for watching television. I took a sharp piece of glass and, hiding under my blankets in my cell, began to saw away at my wrist. Soon I was soaking in sweat and blood, but still I continued to saw away. Eventually I fell into a sort of fitful sleep.

Then I heard a clanging and a banging – I thought I was in Hell. Instead, it was the bolt being drawn across my door. A warder had become worried after calling my name and getting no reply, and had peered into my cell. He probably saved my life, for what it was worth. I was rushed to the prison hospital, where my life was saved by Dr Cooper and his staff. I cannot speak too highly of them.

Dr Cooper explained to me that I had done what I had done because I was suffering from paranoia, an illness of the mind. I was in hospital for quite some time, not only because of my injuries but also because of my mental state. I did a lot of self-analysis as I slowly recovered, even to the extent of making up a riddle about myself:

I thought I was him
I thought I was he
But I am neither
I am the one in between.

My experience led me to do some research into paranoia. I was determined it would never attack and weaken me again. So, for the benefit of others who may suffer from it, this is what it is.

Paranoia is a mental disorder in which the personality gradually deteriorates, and the sufferer often experiences delusions and hallucinations, becomes suspicious and imagines people are persecuting him. I have seen people become paranoid in prison. The length of the prison sentence is not always the deciding factor as some prisoners who suffer from this illness are serving relatively short sentences. But it's fair to say that the longer a person is in prison the greater the likelihood that he will get symptoms of paranoia. Prison life is a strange and abnormal existence, so the possibility of becoming paranoid is far greater in prison than it is in the outside world.

Psychiatrists have told me that a long time spent in prison makes a man's boundaries of interest smaller. This results in his becoming more introvert, which increases the risk of paranoia. One psychiatrist told me that in prison the best safeguard against undue suspicion is to have only one close friend or to keep your number of friends as small as possible. When I think about it, this is good advice, and I would pass it on to any new entries into the world of prison. When a person can confide in another and be confident that his conversation will go no farther, it decreases undue suspicion. Working on the law of averages, the greater the number of people who take part in a conversation, the more chance of a breach of confidence.

Any prison society is made up of a number of strangers massed together, allowing that there is a small minority who already know each other from the outside world. Bearing this situation in mind, it is pretty obvious that there will be good reasons for distrust. The criminal world contains theft, vendetta, murder and various other

124

forms of crime, so most inmates will have good reason to fear betrayal by a fellow con, who may be seeking to curry favour with the prison officials in the hope that he may be granted parole or some other form of reward for supplying information. I am not suggesting that the parole board makes deals with this type of inmate, but this is the sort of reward that informers are seeking.

I often think how nice it would be to live in a non-criminal environment where you could relax and socialize with your neighbours and take part in everyday, normal conversation, without being overly concerned about what you say. You can, and should, be able to socialize as much as possible in prison, and yet still keep within your own circle.

All long-term prisoners go through periods of suffering from loss of identity. To understand this you only need to look at people like Sir Francis Chichester, who, after a year at sea alone on his yacht, could not converse properly on his arrival home. He was suffering a sort of personality disorder brought about by being in total solitude.

There is also the case of the Englishman who was arrested in Russia for spying. He was in solitary confinement in a Russian prison for eighteen months and nearly went insane. He wrote a book about his experiences and his fight against insanity. Now, if you compare his eighteen months in solitary confinement with a life sentence with a recommendation of a minimum of thirty years, much of it in maximum-security, Category A conditions and some of it in solitary confinement, you will get some idea of what I – and others – are up against. It is one hell of a hill to climb, one hell of a battle to fight.

But I have fought it, day by day, month by month, year by year. I know the authorities, the Home Office, won't be happy until they've pushed me over the limit. But they are wasting their time, they won't succeed. I have studied for mental progress and inner calm for many years. It has not been easy. But I believe I have succeeded. I no longer hate people. I bear no malice against the people who put me here – the police and the judge – though I feel they were too severe. Also, since beating my paranoia, I feel I do have many friends, I feel the world and life can hold hope for me. Looking back over those bad years reminds me of an old proverb: 'A thousand years have passed by since yesterday.'

I met kids in Parkhurst whose fathers I knew as young men. One young fellow even asked me what his dad was like. His dad had been in the security block with me many years ago – around 1970 – but had died in prison. All these years later, his son wanted some memories of a dad he barely knew. Sometimes prison life can be bitterly sad.

There are so many young cons in Parkhurst, and that saddens me as well. Not too long back another prisoner said to me about one of the young cons who'd just arrived, 'Watch him. He's a bit of a nutter. He thinks Jack McVitie is his father. He could be after you.' I made a meet with the young con in my cell and told my friends to disappear while I spoke to this young guy. I gave him a cup of tea, let him relax, and then asked him point blank if there was any truth in the rumour that he was the son of Jack the Hat. He assured me it wasn't true. He also assured me that he bore me no malice of any kind. So that was another possible confrontation to cross off my list.

I have met other young kids whose fathers were enemies of mine, yet I have got on well with all of them.

I feel very sorry for young cons. A long-term sentence is not the answer for any young man. It's no wonder that so many of them turn to drugs, particularly to cannabis. Some of them have told me they would crack up, commit suicide, were it not for the relief that cannabis brings.

I myself am very worried about the spread of cannabis – not only in prisons but also in society in general. Cannabis has given many young people who are out of work and redundant a means of finding relaxation from the days of despair. But it also acts as a social bond for those united in adversity – those who see the establishment, and particularly the police, as the enemy. People now enjoy the intrigue and pleasure of smoking joints of cannabis at social gatherings in just the same way as people in America in the 1920s enjoyed their bottles of scotch in Prohibition times.

In the 1960s this country, and in particular London, had illegal gambling which, again, was anti-establishment, and again the intrigue, the element of law-breaking, was a great attraction for those who took part. Gambling in the sixties brought a certain amount of glamour to the London scene – Ron, Charlie and I capitalized on this and made a small fortune. Billy Hill was perhaps the first to spot the enormous potential, the rich pickings, to be made out of people's desire to gamble, often in the seediest of surroundings. Some of the top people in society enjoyed this particular vice as much as those in the lower classes. We witnessed fortunes won and lost in a single evening over the turn of a card. But the fortunes that changed hands this way were nothing to the fortunes being made by the dealers in cannabis and other drugs. There is a ready-made market place for these drugs in prisons and – make no mistake about it – a lot of drugs are smuggled into prisons.

And maybe in some respects it's just as well that they are – for without the calming effect that drugs have on many prisoners, I am sure there could be full-scale anarchy in our gaols.

Every week I get other cons telling me they are going out, going home – either on home leave or going out for good. But that is never the case with me. Years ago other prisoners would never do this to a lifer – they would never speak of going free to a man who was facing years being locked up. But now it seems all forms of respect are diminishing in the world, even in prison. I don't mind other people talking about home leave and freedom, in fact I'm usually pleased for them, but their talk takes its toll on me.

It's even worse for Ron because he lives in a world of total doom, I always come away totally depressed after visiting Ron. How he manages to remain so cheerful living in a place like Broadmoor amazes me. Like me, he relies heavily upon letters and also upon visitors. Without visitors, without the friends who come to see you, you are lost. All kinds of people come to see me and to them all I am very, very grateful.

It's extraordinary the friendships you make in prison. My closest friend at Parkhurst was Pete Gillett. He was in cell 13 and I was in cell 14. On the door is your name and number and religion. They used to write on a board how many years you were in for, but they've stopped doing that now. I don't know why – perhaps to stop you getting even more depressed at the thought of the wasted years.

Pete Gillett is a young man – twenty-six, as I write – from Crawley, in Sussex. He was jailed for six years for conspiracy to rob. His best friend ratted on him to the police to save his own skin.

He was very bitter when I first met him – bitter about his circumstances, bitter about the guy who'd set him up, and bitter about his wife whom he'd split up from. The only good thing in his life seemed to be his son, Liam, whom he idolized.

We became friends and I would like to make it clear that that's all there ever was to it – friendship. It may sound corny but I became the father Pete never really had – he comes from a broken home – and he became the son that I'll never have.

We've helped each other. He forced me to pack up smoking; I forced him to start thinking positively, to develop his interest in music. And as a result he's now a free man. He's become a professional singer and has released a record. He still writes and comes to see me regularly.

It was Pete who saved me from a good hiding one day at Parkhurst. I was watching him play in a football match when, without my noticing it, a gang of about six began creeping up on me. One of them was a distant relation to George Cornell, the guy Ronnie killed, and he must have thought that if he couldn't get Ron, then he'd do me over instead. They were just about to pile in on me when Pete noticed what was happening. He shouted a warning and came running over, boots flying. It was a right old dust-up. Another couple of cons joined in on our side and we finished up the winners – even though Pete did collect a beautiful black eye.

That's the thing about prison life – you need eyes in the back of your head if you are a name prisoner like me. There's always someone who fancies his chances. However, friendships like the one I had with Pete make life more bearable.

I've also made friends, over the years, with other, less likely people. For example, several years ago the padre at Parkhurst was a man called Hugh Searle. He was, and still is, a most compassionate man. Ron and I got to know him well and he was always kind and helpful to any cons in need. On one occasion he took some tobacco from me to a con who was in the punishment block. This was most unusual for a prison padre, but much appreciated. He was much liked by the cons and would sit, quite relaxed, in the cells of some really vicious individuals. Yet he seemed to get along fine with all of them.

I was sad when he left to take up another post in Cambridge. But I feel some of the prison staff and certainly the prison authorities were delighted to see him go – he was far too liberal from their point of view. But, to this day, he stays in touch with Ron and visits him in Broadmoor. He is very much a man from the other side of the fence, and yet still a man I am pleased to count among my friends.

Then there is Watson Lee, a magistrate who lives on the Isle of Wight. He was often summoned to Parkhurst to officiate at the Board of Visitors' hearings – in other words, to deal with offences committed by inmates of the prison.

I first met Watson Lee about fourteen years ago when I was sitting before him on a charge of malicious wounding against another inmate by the name of Roy Grantham. There had been trouble between Grantham and me which started in my cell, which was located, at that time, in the special security block. Grantham had been transferred from Gartree prison because he was such a bully and troublemaker and it was thought that Parkhurst was the only place that could handle him. He had a reputation as someone to be avoided if at all possible. I knew of his reputation and knew that, as I was king of the Parkhurst cons, he would almost certainly make me one of his first targets. But I decided to keep an open mind and made him welcome on his arrival. This was a mistake. I should have paid attention to the prison grapevine which indicated that he was a true bully and would mistake kindness for weakness.

Grantham soon set about tormenting me. I could only tolerate this by suppressing my anger, but I knew my patience would only hold out for so long. The screws knew this as well, so they deliberately made sure we were close together as much as possible. They knew that would guarantee trouble, sooner or later, and give the nasty ones among them the chance to put the boot in on either Grantham or Kray or both.

One of Grantham's habits was to walk into my cell when I was eating a meal. He would pick, at random, some food off my plate and stuff it into his mouth, like a pig. Another of his habits was to lean over the door of the toilet and start a long, boring conversation while I was sitting there. The toilets in Parkhurst have half doors, and so Grantham not only bored me but embarrassed me as well, because during our one-sided conversation he would also stare at me during my act of ablution.

Why didn't I tell him to bugger off and, if that didn't work, why didn't I clock him one? Well, I'm talking here about a man who was half mental. I have never been a coward but with a man like Grantham you have to pick your moment very carefully, otherwise you would get very badly carved up indeed. It had happened to several other cons he'd picked on. Also, he was a big man, over six feet tall. He was a keep-fit maniac, who would drink jugfuls of carrot juice and go around the exercise yard with a towel wrapped round his head and his hands wrapped in bandages like a fighter in training. Everywhere he went he would be shadow-boxing and grunting. Although I could see the humorous side to this, I knew the situation between Grantham and me would end up serious.

The story ended one morning when he came into my cell and started to issue threats because he thought I had slighted him the previous day. His language became more and more abusive and other cons were listening. This was the moment of truth, there was no backing down. Either Reg Kray or Roy Grantham would walk out of that cell. The one who walked out would be king – the other would be flat on his back.

Grantham had a knife which he was waving around, but I never needed weapons. While he was shouting and raving, I picked my moment and smashed him harder in the face than I have ever hit anyone. He went down and I made sure he stayed down. He was badly hurt. Out of loyalty to a fellow con – even though I hated him – I got rid of his knife.

A few days later I was up before the magistrate, Watson Lee, putting up my defence for hitting Grantham. I thought I had a good case and I thought I delivered it well. Mr Lee listened to my case intently. At the end of my submission he looked slightly amused and said, 'It seems that Grantham should be accused, instead of you.' He then paused and said, 'I am awarding you fifty-six days' punishment, which will start today.' I was angry, but I had developed a certain liking for Watson Lee. He had given me a fair hearing. The punishment was a bit excessive – but that's been the story of my life.

This friendly rivalry between myself and Watson Lee continued over the years when there were one or two other bits of bother. Ever since the year of the Grantham affair, Watson Lee and I have sent each other Christmas cards and whenever he was at Parkhurst he would always come and see me in my cell for a chat. We exchanged points of view on a wide range of subjects. He's a man from a totally different world to mine – but a man I admire and a man I am pleased to call a friend.

As for Roy Grantham, in later years he became a supergrass and put many of his friends behind bars. Eventually he committed suicide.

I have always believed that some good will come out of even the worst situations, and the fact that I have made friends with men like Watson Lee and the padre, Hugh Searle, proves this to me.

Funnily enough, it was Watson Lee, I think, who recently sent me a cutting from one of the East End newspapers. Under the headline, 'Publican's Nostalgia for Krays', the writer, a journalist called R. Barry O'Brien, wrote:

> An East End licensee who claims violent crime in his neighbourhood has made people afraid to go out to pubs at night, looked back with nostalgia, yesterday, to the days twenty years ago when the gangster brothers Ronnie and Reggie Kray ruled London's underworld.

He quoted Eddie Johnson, licensee of the Two Puddings public house at Stratford, as saying, 'Compared with some of the villains today the Krays were thorough gentlemen, respected and even admired by many people.

'They were nasty to their own kind, but they left ordinary people alone. Today's villains are nasty to everyone – old, young, middle-aged. They make no distinctions.'

Thank you for the kind words, Mr Johnson. It's what Ron and I have claimed all along, but it's done us no good. The authorities need us as scapegoats.

Parkhurst prison has broken many men in its grim history, but it didn't break me. But right to the end of my stay at Parkhurst the authorities cheated me. I was summoned, early in 1986, to the governor's office and told that I was being sent to Wandsworth prison in London 'for some weeks'. I was furious because there was no reason to send me away and break up the friendship I had built up with Pete Gillett. Besides, in a tough nick like Wandsworth someone like me is a sitting target for any young thug who fancies making a name for himself. I've no worries about defending myself but – as I've learned to my cost over the years – you defend yourself and still finish up in the punishment block.

I protested bitterly but was told, 'It's in your best interests to go to Wandsworth, Reg. The authorities want to try you out in a different environment and then, if you handle it all right, you'll be moved to a softer prison, either Maidstone or Nottingham. And you know what that means. The end of your sentence could be in sight.'

It was all a lie, as it turned out, but I fell for it. I allowed them to take me away from the best friend I ever had. And suddenly I was on the way back to Wandsworth. The last time I had been there was when my beloved Frances and I were engaged. At that time, too, my dear mother and father were alive, and Ronnie and I were the rulers of London's underworld. Twenty-one years had passed since then, and now I was back. But this time it was different. This time there was no Frances, no Mum and Dad. This time I was alone.

The sky above Wandsworth was dirty and grey and typical of London. The little cockney sparrows hovered, quite tame, around my feet, mingling with the London pigeons, as though to welcome me back to Dickensland as a fellow cockney. The little exercise yard at Wandsworth hadn't changed much in all the years; neither had the cells. Yet so much had happened in between.

I thought to myself: it seems as if I have not come far in life. Yet I have walked a fast and hectic pace in between. And even though most of those years had been spent locked away, I had made many friends and learned more about myself than most men do. I had learned how to survive, mentally and physically, against the greatest odds.

Even though I was sad at Wandsworth, I felt my parents and Frances watching over me. It was as though the years had been condensed into the blinking of an eyelid, and I wondered where they had all gone. It would have been easy to be bitter. But I didn't look back in anger because I know there are many others far worse off than me.

No one gave me any bother at Wandsworth. The screws were respectful and so were the other cons. They seemed to sense that I was at a crossroads in my life, that I didn't need any extra hassle. So I was left alone to my thoughts.

The weeks passed quickly and uneventfully – maybe too uneventfully for the prison authorities. Reggie Kray, perhaps, wasn't getting into the kind of trouble they thought he would in his new environment.

132

There was no more talk about a move to a soft prison at Maidstone or Nottingham. Nothing. I began to get suspicious. I should have known I couldn't trust them.

Suddenly one morning my cell door banged open and the screw said, 'Come on, Reg, get your stuff together, you're off again – back to Parkhurst.' Yes, back to Parkhurst – and back to my mate, Pete, but I knew that time was running out and Pete would soon be a free man. What I didn't know was that before Pete was released I would be moved again – this time permanently.

10

Ron: Life in Broadmoor . . .
'Without my drugs I go mad'

In my darker moments I believe I will never get out of Broadmoor. I base this belief on two things. First, a strong gut feeling. Second, information I have received about a conversation between one of the doctors here and one of the administrators. In that conversation it was definitely said, 'Kray will never leave Broadmoor.' I have spoken about this to Dr Tidmarsh, the consultant psychiatrist here who is in charge of me, and he has told me this conversation did not take place. So I don't know. But when I ask Dr Tidmarsh if they will ever release me, he won't give me a definite answer. It's always, 'We'll have to wait and see how things go on.'

I am not criticizing Dr Tidmarsh. He has been very good to me. Sometimes I think I could not have got through the past few years without him. But I believe that if there was any real hope of getting out he would have told me.

They say I am insane. I don't think that I am. Dr Tidmarsh has told my solicitor that my mind is sound enough for me to write this book and he has given me his blessing. I ask you, is he likely to do that to a bloke who's crazy?

I think they could let me out. With the right person to look after me and give me my drugs, I'm sure I would be OK outside. I'd even pay the authorities to supply someone to supervise me at home. I know I wouldn't want to kill again – and I wouldn't want to go back to crime. I'm all right as long as I have my drugs. I take Stemetol capsules four times a day to quieten my nerves. I take Disipal, which is for the side effects caused by the Stemetol, which makes my limbs shake and go out of control. Every fortnight I have an injection of Modicate, which is for schizophrenia. It stops me getting bad dreams and depressions. You see, I know about my drugs. I know

134

what I've got to take and why. I know how to take them. As long as I've got my drugs I could even look after myself.

I will always take them. I know I must. Without my drugs I go mad. I start to imagine that people are plotting against me. I see two people talking and I start to believe that they are planning how they are going to get me. Then I get angry, I feel I have to retaliate, to hurt them for what they are doing. It's a terrible feeling and it's the only time that I feel out of control, like some devil has got inside my brain and is pulling it apart with his bare hands. But the drugs make everything fine. I am calm, I am at peace with the world. I don't bother other people and they don't bother me.

I would just like the authorities to give me a chance of freedom – even if they kept a close watch on me for a time to make sure I was OK. I would like to get out and buy a house in the country with Reg. Somewhere in Suffolk would be ideal. We've always loved Suffolk since we went there as kids. I would just like us to live quietly, and I know that's what Reg wants as well.

Somehow, though, I don't think it would be possible. I think the newspapers and television people and sightseers would probably make our lives hell. I think we'd have to go and live abroad somewhere. I wouldn't mind living in Morocco. Reg and I had one or two lovely visits to North Africa in the old days and we both love the sunshine.

Before I settle down, though, I'd love to travel. I'd love to go to India and China. I've done a lot of reading since I've been here, particularly travel and exploring books, and those two countries really do fascinate me.

Reg and I often talk about going there, particularly when he comes to visit me here. Mind you, it's all we can talk about really. They never give us any privacy. There's always a nurse sitting just a few yards away, and a couple of screws from Parkhurst. For Christ's sake, what the hell could we be plotting? Why do they have to act like Big Brother all the time? It makes me sick.

I'll be very sad if I never get to see India and China. I'd also like to go to Russia, but I'd make that the last place I visited – just in case the KGB have heard of the Krays.

Really, I am quite happy here at Broadmoor. The staff are kind to me and the other patients don't bother me. It's not a prison, it's a hospital. It comes under the Department of Health.

Life here is much easier than in prison, you get a lot more privileges. I've had a much better time than Reg – he's really suffered. Some people have said that I deliberately got myself sent here, that I acted violent and mad on purpose because I knew that Broadmoor would be much softer. It's not true.

When we went down in 1969 I was sent to Durham gaol and Reg was sent to Parkhurst. We missed each other a lot, we've always been very close. My mother and other people campaigned to get us back together and in 1972 I was transferred to Parkhurst. Life was OK until we got a new governor who took a dislike to me.

I was very friendly with another con called Peter Gattrell. He was terribly upset one day because his mother had died of cancer. I wanted to show my respect to my friend's mother, so I put in an application to send a wreath to her funeral. When you're a Category A con you've got to put in an application for just about everything except a crap, and even for that they give you an escort.

This governor called me up to his office. I could see from the look on his face that there was going to be trouble. 'Who are these flowers for?' he said.

'They're for Pete Gattrell's mother,' I said. 'I want your permission to send them.'

'Well, Mr Kray', he said, 'permission is refused.' Just like that, the bastard.

I swore at him and that cost me seven days in chokey (solitary confinement). I would have killed him if I could have got to him, but the warders stopped me.

After that it was all trouble and fights. I just didn't care any more. All I could see was years and years in front of me as a Category A con, and when you're an 'A' prisoner life is very hard. You're under constant supervision, your visitors are restricted, there are very few perks, and you're under threat all the time – from the warders and from the other cons. It's worse than living in the jungle. I just don't know how Reg stood it all those years.

There was one really bad fight with another con – I can't even remember what it was about, probably nothing important, but in prison just one silly remark can spark off a full-scale brawl. I remember I beat him up badly, and after that they certified me insane and said I was being moved to Broadmoor.

Another con at Parkhurst, Nobby Clark, who'd done a spell in Broadmoor, said to me that I'd like it here. 'It can be heaven or hell in Broadmoor,' he said. 'If you get into trouble there, it's hell. But if you stay out of trouble, it's heaven.' Well, I've stayed out of trouble and if it hasn't exactly been heaven, it could have been a lot worse.

I never get any trouble. The other patients know who I am, and unless I invite them to be a friend, they keep clear of me and only pass the time of day.

You have to have one or two close friends, even in a place like this. My best friend here at the moment is called Charlie Smith. I call him Fearless Charlie 'cause he ain't frightened of anything. He's twenty-seven and a cockney. He's serving two life sentences, one for murder and one for manslaughter. He's been here now for nearly seven years. Like a lot of murderers, you can't really believe he's done what they say. He's a lovely, gentle bloke. He's also a brilliant guitar player and singer – he often sings and plays for me. A record company is hoping to bring their gear into Broadmoor to record him singing some of his songs. They would like to put them out and I'm sure if they did he would become a big star.

He is visited regularly by a young female student from Sussex. She is a lovely, quiet, intelligent girl. She takes a genuine interest in Charlie. We all need someone to care about us.

I have one regular female visitor – my wife, Elaine. Yes, I have a wife and a legal one at that. She began by being a penfriend to Reg, but then she started writing to me. She started to visit me and we got on really well. There's no sex or anything like that. It's not allowed. But we just built up a good relationship. She was lonely and needed a friend to talk to, and so was I.

Two years ago we got married here in Broadmoor and the *Sun* paid Elaine several thousand pounds for the exclusive story and pictures. I was amazed that they let a newspaper photographer inside Broadmoor to take pictures of the ceremony, but they did. I would have thought they wouldn't have done that if I was the complete looney some people say I am. It also goes to prove what I was saying about life being much easier here than in prison.

Elaine is a lovely girl, both to look at and in personality. She has

137

two kids, teenagers, a boy called Andrew and a girl called Debbie. They both call me Dad when they come to see me at Broadmoor occasionally, and when they write to me. I am very fond of them and their mother. I have told Elaine, though, that if I do get out of Broadmoor, I won't be going to live with her and the kids. I shall go and live with Reg. We'll end our lives as we started, together.

I shall have so much to see and do in my remaining years, I won't have the time to devote to looking after a family. They will always be looked after financially and I will visit them regularly, but I won't be able to live with them. I've got to spend the rest of my life with Reg and doing my travelling – though they can come and stay with Reg and me whenever they like. This may be a bit hard for other people to understand, but Elaine and the kids understand, and that's all that really bothers me. I couldn't really give a toss what anyone else thinks.

People like Elaine keep people like me alive. Penfriends and visitors are often the only things that keep some prisoners going. Reg has dozens of penfriends all over the world – some of them very famous – and he loves to write letters. Last Christmas he got something like three hundred cards. I bet that's more than the Prime Minister. I got about two hundred and fifty. Of course, you also get a lot of letters from complete nutters, but you just ignore them.

Visitors are very important, particularly here where you can have visitors for four hours a day. Visitors really kill the time for you, give you some contact with the outside world. I'm lucky. Apart from Elaine and the kids, and Reg, I get visits from some of the old firm, from my brother Charlie, and also from some very famous people in other fields. One of my most loyal friends has been Wilf Pine, who owns a record company.

Living conditions here aren't too bad. The place itself is bloody grim. It was built in about 1870 in bloody awful red-coloured bricks. I'll never forget the day I arrived. The roads leading here are really pretty and lined with big trees. I remember driving up a hill called Chaplains Hill, and then suddenly seeing this terrible-looking building in front of me. I felt really depressed.

Inside it's just as bad. Everything is old-fashioned, everything needs a bloody good paint. But the people who work here are kind, and that's the main thing. There are one or two who try to wind up some of the patients, really get them going and starting fights. But you always get cruel bastards wherever you go. They don't try it on me. I am quite happy here – as happy as it's possible to be when you're in a lunatic asylum and don't really think you are a looney.

They've given me a nice room here. It's not very big, about the size of a prison cell. It's painted blue. I have a bed, of course, a writing table, a colour television and a cassette player and radio. The cassette player is very important to me. I listen to a lot of music. My favourite is *Madame Butterfly*. I also like to listen to the radio – especially at night when all the lights have been turned out. I love to listen to music on the radio and sometimes talks and plays. I don't watch the television much. It's all violence – violence on the news and violence in films. Christ knows what today's kids are going to grow up like, with all this violence.

I read a lot, mainly travel books, though I have read the life stories of people like Winston Churchill, Genghis Khan and Attila the Hun. I never read fiction, and I never read books about Reg and myself because they are full of so many lies that they make me depressed and angry.

I get up every morning at seven and clean my room out. It's the only real work I do – I have never believed in work, particularly manual work. They pay me £10 a week to keep my room clean. It helps to pay for cigarettes and the non-alcoholic lager which I like. I smoke too much, I know, but that's because I get very bored. The days here are long and when the weather is bad they pass slowly. Reg used to be a chainsmoker but he has now given it up completely. I admire him for that, but I don't think I have got the willpower to do it myself.

Before breakfast I also do some exercises in the corridor. I try to keep myself as fit as possible but it's difficult here because there is no gymnasium.

We have visitors between 10 a.m. and 12 p.m. and someone comes to see me most days. I am grateful for that because visitors make the morning pass more quickly. If I don't have visitors I go for walks along the corridors of Broadmoor. Sometimes I go out into the grounds, though I am restricted where I can go. After all this time I

139

still don't have full ground leave – I still can't go walking wherever I want. I find that annoying.

We have lunch and then more visitors between 2 and 4 pm. Then we have tea. Lights go out at 9.

My visitors are made welcome. The visitors' room here is not very comfortable, it's like a waiting room at a railway station, but my visitors can have tea or coffee and biscuits. They don't have to pay – I have an account with one of the nurses which I settle up every week. I don't expect gifts, there is nothing I need, but if anyone brings in a hundred fags – John Player Specials – then I am pleased.

If people are wondering where I get the money from to pay for my luxuries, like my fags and lager and my suits, let me kill another lie they tell about Reg and me – we do *not* have any illegal business interests still operating. In fact, we don't have any real business interests at all.

But there's still a bit of money in the pot – we lost a lot when we were in business, we were cheated out of a lot, but we managed to keep a bit. Charlie keeps an eye on that. We also get a share of the royalties from one or two books which we have written about ourselves, newspapers and magazines pay us well for occasional articles they write about us, and we've been negotiating one or two deals with film companies who want to make films about our lives.

We also get a bit of revenue from people who sell T-shirts with our names on, and calendars and things like that. It's not a lot, and it's not a big racket like some national newspapers claimed.

Once again, a pack of lies has been written about us. The mud sticks and it makes it harder for Reg and me – especially for Reg. But if people are making money using our names, why shouldn't we get a bit? We've still got family and friends to look after. We've still got expenses. We do not make a fortune, but it's amazing that we make anything at all. After all, it's now twenty years since we were put away. Who'd have thought the Krays would still be famous after all this time? When we do get out we won't be rich men, but we won't be paupers either. Reg and I will never starve and we'll never need to go the wrong side of the law again, either.

I keep myself clean, my hair is always washed and cut, and I am the smartest man in the whole of Broadmoor. I believe that if you

140

start to let yourself go, if your standards drop, then you've had it. You've got to keep up appearances, keep up your morale. That's why I still get my suits handmade and sent in from outside. That's why I wear a clean shirt every day. I was the top man once. They used to call me the Colonel. And I still feel I am the top man, even though I am not a gangster any more.

I think I have adapted to life here well, although it's a different life from Reg's. Broadmoor may not be like an ordinary hospital, but we are still treated more like hospital patients here than like criminals. I'm proud of the way I have come to terms with my life. Only today I received a letter from dear Hugh Searle, now a vicar but for fourteen years the chaplain at Parkhurst prison. I know Hugh won't mind my quoting from it. He wrote: 'It was good to see you the Saturday before last. I was so pleased you manage to keep your spirits up against all the odds. That is a great tribute to your strength and determination to let nothing finally get you down, and never to lose heart.'

I, in my turn, am proud that a man like him should give up his time to come to visit me.

I was quite touched, too, to receive a copy of his sermon for that coming Sunday. In it he said: 'In prison I learnt two valuable and illuminating lessons. One was that it was not much use if I just shouted at people, telling them how to get right with God. The other was that one can stumble across courage, generosity and deep faith in God in the most unlikely places – finding diamonds in the dirt is one of life's greatest and most glorious discoveries.' Were Reggie and I among his diamonds? I guess not, but it's a nice thought.

One of the things I do here to pass the time is write poetry. Here's a poem I wrote which just about sums up the way I feel. It's called 'The Lifer'.

> The years roll by.
> You can see winter turn
> To summer by the sky.
> Home seems far away.
> How much longer behind these walls must we stay?
> I say a prayer for my fellow men behind bars

Who gaze up at freedom and the stars.
We think things are bad for us,
But there are crippled children who make no fuss.

Let us waken from our sleep
And be as free as sheep.
Let our hearts soar high.
As high as birds in the sky,
As we think of being free,
As at long last the end of the road
We can see.

Postscript

Since I wrote this chapter, Elaine has told me that she wants a divorce. She cannot stand the strain of living this way any more. I have agreed to her request. She has my blessing. It was a great blow, but just another chapter in the saga of the Kray twins. I call it 'The Stage of Life':

We are all actors on a stage and, whatever parts we have been given, we must play it through to the best of our ability and not grumble at the part that has been given to us. It is not up to us to question the part we have been given. It is up to us to play it to the best of our ability.

You will find there are people with worse parts to play than us, but we must see it through to the end, the evening of life, until the curtain goes down – and hope that we will get a worthy ovation.

We must consider the other actors on the stage, our friends and the people we love. We must not take for granted the good things about ourselves that God has given us and the beauty that is around for all of us to see.

There is none so blind as those who will not see and none so deaf as those who will not hear.

11

Reg: Life in Gartree

Christmas 1986 was a great one for me. Ridiculous, isn't it? In the nick yet still I can say I had a great time. I was back in Parkhurst after my spell at Wandsworth. I was back with my small circle of friends, in particular Pete Gillett. And I still had in my mind the promise that, if all went well at Wandsworth (which it had), I would be considered for a move to Maidstone or Nottingham. That would not only make my life more bearable but would also bring closer the day of my final release. Good enough reasons to be happy to be back – even in a hellhole like Parkhurst.

On Christmas Eve a friendly screw brought us in some turkey, with roast potatoes, peas and gravy, some Christmas pudding, plus a couple of bottles of wine and a drop of the hard stuff. Five of us had a really good meal in my cell and then Pete got out his guitar and began to play and sing. We all sat around, singing songs, having a quiet drink and reliving better times in our lives. We even gave each other small gifts. It was a magical time and that feeling of goodwill continued well into January.

Then the whispers began on the prison grapevine, that amazing source of information for all prisoners. The word was that Reggie Kray was on the move. Everyone was pleased for me, but I had my doubts. I had a gut feeling that if I was about to be moved, it was going to be a bad move – otherwise the prison authorities would have kept me in touch. As it was, I hadn't heard a word from them. I could smell a rat, a double-cross.

Then, at just after nine at night on Wednesday, 21 January 1987, my cell door was opened and three screws walked in.

One of them said, 'The governor wants to see you – right away. and get all your things together, you're being moved to another cell.'

143

So this was it. I was on the way out of Parkhurst. All the signs were there – the summons by the governor, the move to another cell – a kind of spartan departure lounge – prior to being shipped out. And the whole thing happening at that time of night – there could be no other reason. I suddenly knew this would be the last time I would see my cell at Parkhurst – and the last time I would see my mate Pete for some time. He still had a few more months to serve.

I said to be the screws, 'OK, I'll not cause any fuss. But I want a word with Pete before I go.'

One of the screws said that wasn't possible. So I told him, 'If I don't see Pete I'm not moving from this fucking cell.'

They knew I meant it and they didn't want any bother, so one of them went next door and unlocked Pete's cell. He came out straightaway. He'd heard the row and knew that something was up.

It was a very emotional moment. Pete was the best mate I'd ever had, apart from my brother Ron, and now we were being split up. And I was going God knows where.

I said goodbye to Pete, shook his hand, kissed him on the forehead and said, 'Stay in touch.' Then I was taken to the governor's office where two assistant governors were waiting.

'Where am I going?' I asked them.

They told me they thought I was going to Maidstone and I asked if Pete could be moved to Ford, an open prison near Arundel in Sussex, where the footballer George Best had spent some time. I thought he would be better and happier at Ford rather than, say, Northeye, another open prison in Sussex where there had been some trouble in recent months. In fact, I was destined for Gartree, another maximum-security prison, in Leicestershire, and Pete went to Northeye. Once again the prison authorities had done the dirty on me.

Shortly after our farewell on that fateful night in January, Pete sent a letter to my brother Ron. I was sent a copy of that letter by Ron and I'm sure that Pete won't mind me repeating it in this book. He wrote:

Dear Ronnie,

I feel desperately upset as I write this letter. About half an hour ago, the cell door opened and I walked out and saw Reg and three screws. He was being taken away, where we do not know.

The fact it's happened the way it has indicates to me that it's a bad move. Please God I'm wrong.

My heart feels heavy, Ronnie. I dread Reggie's fate. If he was off to Maidstone, I cannot see why he was ghosted out tonight in this fashion.

His face – though he was trying to look calm and strong – will stay in my memory for ever. I'm terribly upset by this. I can't begin to put my emotions down on paper. I just hope, being his twin, you'll understand why I feel so lonely and totally helpless to comfort him. The anguish on his face made me cry like a baby. Today, to make it worse, we had an argument. It makes for no big deal, but it has sickened me that, on our last day, we should argue.

I will try to find out where Reg has gone before I post this to you in the morning, Ron. Tonight we sat together, ate our last meal, and talked about you, Charlie, Reg and me, as though we knew it was our last meal – though no one had indicated as much.

Reg will not be happy until I am out of here. He feels that someone will make a move on me in his absence. I can handle myself, but it won't stop him worrying. There are some dirty slags in here.

I suppose it was humane of the screws to open my cell to let us see each other, talk, shake hands, and say goodbye. Reg kissed my forehead and was gone. I can't remember being so hurt inside for a long time.

I will end now, Ronnie, as I just don't know what to say. The more I try, the worse I get. I've never had a friend like Reg before, so it is hard to talk at this moment.

Goodnight and God bless.

Peter

As it turned out, it was a couple of days before Pete found out where I had gone. Even my brother Charlie wasn't told until I had been gone for several hours.

I found Pete's concern very touching. I was angry that, despite the promise I was given, he was taken to Northeye prison in Sussex. But I am pleased that he served his time out there without any incidents and he is now a free man. I hope he will bear in mind all the advice I gave him during our time together. If he does then he will remain a free man. I am confident he will.

Meanwhile, at 8.15 the next morning, 22 January, after a night in which I barely slept a wink, I was handcuffed and put in a prison van

145

with a police escort and driven away from Parkhurst for the last time. It was the end of a traumatic time in my life, and my long stay in Parkhurst, if nothing else, should now qualify for a place in *The Guinness Book of Records*!

We crossed the Solent by ferry – with me, of course, still locked inside the prison van – and then began our mainland journey. I asked the screws with me where we going but they would not tell me. I was angry. I never spoke another word for the entire journey. We kept driving until 1.15, when we arrived – not at Maidstone, not at Nottingham, but at Gartree prison, which is near Market Harborough in Leicestershire.

Gartree, in case the prison officials at Parkhurst are not aware of it, is in a different bloody county to Nottingham prison, and it's a bloody sight farther away from Maidstone – in my case, several years away in terms of my freedom.

They call Gartree the Village and, from a distance it may look like a collection of buildings such as you would get in a village. But that, believe me, is the only connection. It is a much more modern building, or series of buildings, than Parkhurst – and it is built in the American style of prison. Long, low buildings set in the middle of acres and acres of flat, ploughed fields, without a tree in sight and some way from the main road. It's an escaper's nightmare – not that I had any intention of trying to escape.

I was desperately unhappy when I arrived, but a con I had never met before had put some flowers in my cell to brighten it up. A thoughtful gesture. I have to confess that, although I am bitterly disappointed about being moved here and not to Notting-ham or Maidstone, life at Gartree is pleasanter than it is at Parkhurst.

At first I was rushing round like a madman, trying to get everything done, trying to let everyone know where I was. But a con I befriended early on, Paul Hanmore, pointed out that I had plenty of time to do all the things I wanted – several more years, in fact. Paul also said that *any* move from the Isle of Wight to the mainland should be regarded as a favourable move in terms of eventual freedom, but I'm not so certain about that.

It's very clean here and I haven't seen a single cockroach since I arrived – Parkhurst, Wandsworth and the Scrubs are crawling with them. They are disgusting creatures that make prison life even more unpleasant.

There are five wings here, plus the main security block, E Wing, which is where I am. Still regarded as a security risk! A, B, C and D are all normal location wings. Then there's F Wing, which is the Rule 43 wing – that contains sex offenders, child killers, grasses and other cons who want or need protection and segregation from the normal cons. One or two sex offenders and the like are scattered around in the other normal blocks, but most cons prefer to ignore them. No one likes these monsters, but if anyone has a go at them, he just gets nicked himself, and it's hardly worth getting into more bother than you've already got. However, as is well known, sex criminals and the like occasionally have 'accidents'.

The screws deliberately scatter a few nonces (sex offenders) on the normal wings, because they are the ones who will always grass on anything and anyone, just to keep in the officers' good books. The penalty for anyone caught grassing is, of course, a bloody good hiding.

There are no sex offenders or the like in E Wing. We are the so-called hard men of the prison and we simply wouldn't tolerate them. Among those in here with me is the cop killer 'Hate 'Em All' Harry Roberts. He'll have his own story to tell one day.

The cells here are small – 7 feet by 8 feet – and they always seem to be either boiling hot or freezing cold. But at least they are single cells. And there's another amazing luxury – you are allowed to operate your own light switch! You can turn your own cell light on and off when *you* want, not when the screws want. That may sound ridiculous, but for me, after years and years without the right, turning on my own light switch is a privilege I value.

We are also allowed certain other luxuries like curtains, bed-spread and tablecloth to make the room a little more comfortable. The beds are bolted to the floor so, apart from the table and the chair, you can't do much in the way of altering the layout.

I spend a lot of the time here drawing and painting. Besides keeping myself fit, it more or less dominates my life. I've tried many hobbies over the years to occupy my mind. I even tried astronomy. That idea was suggested to my by Paul Wrightson, one of our QCs at the Old Bailey. I enjoyed it for a while but now I find painting and writing more absorbing. Keep fit, of course, is my real obsession, and because of it I now have a good physique for a man of my age. There is no fat on me at all, but there is still a lot of good, firm muscle.

Pictures of me appeared in the *Sunday Mirror* not too long ago. They were taken at Parkhurst by another con who'd had a small camera smuggled in to him by a relation. The idea was that this con would take some pictures of me in the gym, lifting weights and so on, and then we would sell them to a Sunday newspaper. That's exactly what happened, though as usual I got ripped off. The paper paid a lot of money for the pictures – but I never received a penny. Once again someone else has done a bunk with my share of the loot. Years ago that would have meant instant retribution, but now I no longer worry. The people who cheat me will be the losers themselves in the long run. Life has a great way of evening things out, as I've discovered to my own cost.

But I was pleased with the photographs because they proved to the world that I am still in great shape physically – better than I've been for years. Mentally I'm still in good shape too. And I was pleased that the Kray name is still big enough, even after all these years, to guarantee a picture spread in one of our biggest-selling Sunday papers.

There's a tough young con in here whom I'll call John. He's got a heart of gold, but he's the noisiest, most aggressive bastard I've ever met. I wanted to point out to him – gently – that it's not a good thing to be too noisy and aggressive. So I showed him the *Desiderata* which hangs in my cell. I pointed out the words: 'Avoid loud and aggressive people – they are a vexation to the spirit.' I waited for his reaction. John looked, then said, 'Too fucking true, Reg. I smack people like that in the jaw.'

Two other cons in Gartree achieved fame when they made a spectacular escape. John Kendall and Sydney Draper were whisked away by a hijacked helicopter which landed in the prison grounds. Kendall was rearrested in February 1988, but Draper is still on the run – and good luck to him. I feel for men like this. I understand their desperation.

But I feel most for the young cons – some of them barely more than boys, young men with so little hope – who are being sent to prison on long sentences and packed into a system which is no longer big enough to accommodate them. I ask myself why so many of them finish up in prison.

And invariably they are doing time for crimes of violence. For much of this I blame the violence shown on the television screen, especially during the hours when children are able to watch. The violence of the Rambo films, for example, must have an influence on young minds. You've only to watch young offenders in prison as they watch films of this kind – they see themselves in the role of hero or anti-hero. And what about Michael Ryan, the gunman who ran amok at Hungerford in Berkshire, dressed like Rambo and armed with a Kalashnikov rifle like the kind used by Rambo? Don't tell me that this unfortunate individual did not at some stage have his mind corrupted by screen violence.

I have also seen rapists glued to the television as they watch films and plays in which women are the victims. I have seen one infamous killer of women who would only watch films containing gory or violent scenes. He seemed to relate the violence on the screen to his own acts of violence. Anyone who believes that the media cannot influence young minds is a fool.

I know the government is at long last showing concern about the violence portrayed on British television. But they must do more than show concern, they must act dramatically, otherwise our prisons will be packed even tighter with violent and dangerous criminals. And the toy manufacturers should cease to make violent toys – replica guns and knives and so forth. This may sound strange coming from someone like me, but too late I have learned the lessons of an early life of violence.

The more violence is portrayed on the screen the more violence there will be in the streets. And gone are the days when the victims of a gangster's violence were other villains. Nowadays anyone is fair game – especially the very young and the very old.

I still get dozens of letters here, some of them really touching. Just before my birthday on 24 October last year I received a letter from a man called Vincente Rossano, who was living in Harrow in Middlesex. I am sure he won't mind my quoting from it.

Hi there Reg,
    You won't remember me, but you helped me and my late wife back

149

in 1967. We were in a pub in Whitechapel, opposite the London hospital. It was night-time and you and your brothers came in with your mates. You bought everybody a drink and you asked me what I was sad and upset about. I said my wife and I had been sleeping rough. You said, don't worry.

Well, to cut a long story short, about an hour later one of your mates said to go with him. He took us to a flat in Arberry Road, Mile End, and told us we now had a furnished flat with a month's rent paid in advance, and not to worry any more.

He said you had arranged it. Well, I can't ever explain how I felt that night, I was so grateful for somewhere for me and my wife to stay in warmth and security.

I also got a job putting cats' eyes in the roads, good money in those days, which I also think you arranged. I have never forgotten this kindness you showed me.

Three years ago my wife died but now, on the anniversary of her death (16 October) I remember back all those years ago to a cold and rainy night in Whitechapel.

So, happy birthday, Reg, and may God have compassion and release you very soon. You have paid your debt to society. I am now in a bed and breakfast hotel, but one day I will shake your hand and repay the favour.

Yours faithfully,
Vince

Letters like that, for obvious reasons, mean a lot to Ron and me. It shows that many people haven't forgotten us – for good rather than bad reasons.

Our true friends haven't forgotten either. Names like Alec Steen, Geraldine Charles, Henry Berry, Dave Gannaway and Ken Stallard may not mean anything to you, but to me and Ron they have given a priceless gift – friendship – when the rest of the world no longer wanted to know. And there are others I must mention – Mick Bartley, Rocky Lee, Vinnie Manson, Tony Knightley, Alf Berkeley, Wayne Oldyer, Paul Hanmore, Mick Archer, Guy Smith, Joe Lee and Harry Gracer. My apologies for taking up time and space, but these people are important to me and Ron. There are others, of course, but I can't mention them all. I hope they will forgive me, but they will know who they are and they will know how precious they are to the Kray twins.

So my new life at Gartree goes on. No one bothers me here – they know better than that. Most of the cons I associate with are good blokes, and the screws are decent enough.

How long I will be here God only knows. Maybe by the time this book is published I will be the guest of Her Majesty at some other fine penal establishment. One thing, and one thing only, is for certain – I still won't be a free man. Not unless miracles really do happen. But, whatever happens, just like the Isle of Wight, this is one part of the country I don't ever want to see again.

12

Ron: Painting and Poetry

Poetry might seem a strange hobby for one of the men who once ruled London's underworld – a man convicted of murder. And yet I find, along with reading and listening to music, that writing poetry is one of the things that relaxes my mind most of all.

I'm not saying my poetry is any good when you compare it to the great poets. Over the years I've written dozens of poems and I've slung a lot of them away because even I didn't think they were good enough. But it's not a competition. Life isn't a competition any more. And I'm glad, because it means that I can sit down and write my poems, lose myself completely in my imagination, and not give a damn about what anyone else thinks. It pleases me, and that's all that's important. It stills my mind.

I'm not going to take this opportunity to ram poem after poem down your throats. In any case, you'd probably keep turning over the pages. After all, you're not exactly a captive audience, are you? But I would like to show you three of my poems – three that mean a lot to me. The first one is called 'The King' and I was inspired to write it after listening to a programme on the radio about polar bears. The programme painted such pictures in my mind that when it was over I decided to write a poem about this brave and isolated animal. I could see similarities between the polar bear and my brother Reg and me. Hunted and alone in a wilderness, but still the king.

> *The King*
> The winter is cold
> Now the polar bear is bold.
> It is his, this wilderness,
> It is his stronghold.

The vast stretches of snow,
The long walks
That by the ice are made slow.
He is the King,
It is his wilderness,
This thing.
The vast stretches of snow,
He will be on the watch
For the hunter with the bow.
But he is the King,
He will smash
The hunter with his sling.
Why not? It is his,
This wilderness, this thing.
He is the King.

I hope you like that.

Another poem I like I called 'The Blind Boy'. Milton once wrote a poem with the same title but, as he and I are unlikely to be in competition, I don't think he would mind if I borrowed his title. My poem is about a friend I had when I was much younger. He went blind, but he was bloody brave about it. I didn't write this poem at the time; as a matter of fact I didn't write it until 1986. I was just sitting in my room at Broadmoor one night when I thought about my friend and started to write my dedication to him.

The Blind Boy
His eyes could see no more,
But he did not think he was poor.
He could feel the shake of his friends' hands
And hear the music from the great bands.
God was his guide; and, most of all
He still had his pride.
He always had the memory of his Mother's face,
And remembered her dignity and grace.
He could see no more, but the memory
Of his friends' faces he would have in store.
God was his guide; and, he knew that He
Would show him the way and had never lied.

153

And, finally, a short poem called 'The New Moon' which was inspired simply by looking out of my window here at Broadmoor one night and seeing this really beautiful new moon. I sat and stared at it, marvelling at its beauty, even as it shone on an ugly building like Broadmoor, and I began to write.

The New Moon
The New Moon is pale blue
And beautiful,
Like the flowering bluebell
In the morning dew.
This is God's beauty
That to all of us is free and true,
And is meant for all God's children
Not just the few.

It is in the sky
So far away and high,

When people say they believe in God
Need we ask why?

So there we are – just a sample of my poetry – and, of course, you've seen a couple of other poems of mine elsewhere in this book. I hope you've found maybe one that you enjoyed. As I say, this is one of the things I find is good for me. It helps pass the endless days.

With me it's poetry and with Reggie, apart from his fanaticism for keep fit and the endless letters he writes, the other big interest in his life – and this may surprise you – is painting. Like me, he may not be ready to take on the Old Masters, but he enjoys it.

His first attempt at painting was for a charity in aid of the Addenbrookes Children's Liver Transplant Fund. Addenbrookes is a hospital at Cambridge where they specialize in work on liver transplants. Reg heard about a man called Peter Maguire and his wife who were desperately trying to raise cash for their little girl Julie, who needed a liver transplant. So he wrote to Mr Maguire and offered to do a painting for him which he could sell to raise money for Julie. Peter Maguire was thrilled, one thing led to another, and in the end Reggie had about thirty other prisoners at Parkhurst and other prisons doing paintings and drawings. He also got me to donate a matchstick model of an old gypsy cart. Reg did a painting of two boxers in the ring and that alone was sold for £430 to a man called Arthur Haines. The whole auction, held at a hotel in Cambridge and called 'Rogues' Gallery', made several thousands pounds.

I read a newspaper quote from Peter Maguire after he'd received all those paintings from Reggie and the other cons at Parkhurst. Mr Maguire said, 'Parkhurst is a very forbidding place and security is very tight. But you don't think what the prisoners have done – they are just people. Although they are behind bars they are not animals – they have gone out of their way to help us.' He also said, 'They don't benefit in any way, other than the satisfaction of knowing they are helping a charity and helping children. I think some of their work is rather good.'

Reggie then went on to do other paintings for charity, including one for the Venture Boxing Club for boys in Liverpool, which had been burned down.

Reggie has always been a lover of painting. His favourite painter is Constable, who lived in our favourite area of Suffolk. His favourite film is *The Agony and the Ecstasy*, which is about the great painter Michälangelo and starred Charlton Heston.

I think his interest in painting began many years ago when we ran Esmerelda's Barn in Knightsbridge. Two of our regular customers were famous painters – Francis Bacon and Lucian Freud. Both used to give Reg a lot of advice and encouragement with his painting. They also both used to play *chemin de fer* and would win and lose thousands of pounds at one sitting.

The police at Portsmouth wanted to buy one of Reg's paintings to hang in their mess, but their superintendant refused them permission. That upset Reg.

Over the years Reggie has raised thousands of pounds for charity – and I've raised a few bob myself – and it's all been done from inside either Parkhurst or Broadmoor.

So that's another side of Reggie Kray – and if you ever look in his prison cell, you will see a photo of Julie Maguire, the little girl from Gosport whose life he helped save.

When he's a free man, look out for Reggie Kray the painter, and also for Reggie Kray the songwriter, because his friendship with Pete Gillett inspired Reg to write a song which Pete hopes one day to put on record. Song lyrics sometimes don't look much on paper but I've heard Pete singing this song on tape and, believe me, it's bloody good. It's called 'Masquerade' and these are the words, as written by my brother.

Masquerade
I understand it's a masquerade;
Life's path tells me this story.
I know and understand,
But I say: Why should it be me?
Maybe I thought I was exempt of life's problems,
It's just human nature.
That we just have to say: 'Yes, it happened to me,'
I do not know why.
I'll hold you no grudge,
But remember it could have been me,
Holding you close tonight,
But it is he.
Physical or in my mind he is there,
And I'm sad to say, but since that day
There are many who have taken your place.
Maybe we have both grown up and apart
And though it is difficult to comprehend,
This is the way the story must end.
It's just a masquerade!

13

Reg: Just a Thought

Just a thought. Sometimes I wake early from a deep sleep and lie in the quietness of my cell. I can hear the beating of my heart and I think of a roaring sea crashing against the rocks on a barren beach somewhere in my favourite area of Cornwall. And I equate each roar of the sea along with the heavy beat of my heart . . .

That's all we're left with now – our thoughts. Ron in Broadmoor, me in Gartree.

Ron believes that he will never get out. I have been told that I will serve at least twenty-seven of the thirty years I was sentenced to. In my time I've been in prison with rapists, murderers and terrorists. Nearly all of them are now free men.

Ron and I killed one man each. Both of the men we killed were violent men, gangsters. One, by his own admission, had already killed another man. The other had shot and wounded at least one man and would almost certainly have killed another – given the time and the chance he would have killed me. For that we have spent more than twenty years in captivity, often treated worse than wild animals.

Ron and I will never kill again. We will never go back to the underworld. We're too old for that now. We're dinosaurs. We'd be eaten alive by the new young men who now control British crime in conjunction with the American Mafia. These men deal in drugs and death and make millions, but are rarely caught.

It's a different world now to what it was in 1969 when we went down. It's a different criminal world too – it's far more deadly. Then it was dog eat dog – criminals waging war against other criminals. Old ladies didn't get attacked by vicious young thugs in those days.

Young girls didn't get raped in broad daylight. Coppers didn't get kicked and punched and spat on at football matches. There was a kind of respect for people in those days. The streets were safe places to walk then – but not any more if what I read and hear is true.

I don't think even I would feel safe in the streets of London any more. In fact, neither Ron nor I would return to London. All we want now is the chance to enjoy some peace and quiet and solitude in the years that are left to us.

But will we get it? We've paid the penalty – but will we ever get our freedom?

You've read our story now, so now you will know us a little better than you did before. You must judge for yourselves. We did bad things, yes, we've admitted it. But were we that bad that we must continue to suffer this inhuman treatment year after year after year? Is there no compassion?

I once saw these words on a card pinned to another prisoner's cell wall: 'I would hate, old, grey and gnarled, and lying on my death bed, to look at the crack – ever increasing on the ceiling – and cry to myself: God, I wish I had.'

Often I've looked at the cracks in the ceiling of my prison cell and cried to myself: 'God, I wish I *hadn't*.'

I appeal to the authorities – release us. Hasn't justice been done? And hasn't justice been seen to have been done? Look at the facts. Look at the wasted years. Then come and look at a broken man in Broadmoor and a despairing man at Gartree.

I think you will know the answer.

Fred Dinenage: A Final Word

I have spoken with officials at the Home Office who tell me it is 'unlikely' that the Parole Review Board will consider the case of Reg Kray until 1991. They also feel it is 'unlikely' that he will be released until he has served at least twenty-seven of the thirty years to which he was originally sentenced.

I have also seen the Mental Health Review Tribunal's psychiatric report on Ron Kray, dated 9 June 1987. In it Dr D. Tidmarsh, the consultant psychiatrist at Broadmoor, concludes:

> Ronald Kray, now aged 53, is a chronic paranoid schizophrenic. In what for him is the unstressful environment of Broadmoor, his illness does not become florid and its symptoms are more or less controlled by medication.
>
> I am sure, however, that he would relapse if he were under stress, as he would be if he were returned to prison. As he is the first to admit, he can no longer stand the pace of prison or, I believe, the competition from other, younger prisoners, and in that environment he would deteriorate rapidly, with the risk of further violence.
>
> In these circumstances I recommend that he should stay in Broadmoor.

Ron Kray tells me he is 'satisfied' with this report and 'very happy' that he will not be returned to prison.

Reg Kray, in contrast, is 'very unhappy, frustrated and angry' at the attitude of the Home Office. There are those who believe he is justified in his feelings.

Acknowledgements

Many people, in different ways, have helped me in the writing and publication of this book. I would especially like to mention Susan Hill, Geraldine Charles, Joe Pyle, John Buckland, Bob Deamer, Pete Gillett, Stephen Gold, my wife and family, and – of course – the twins themselves.

Fred Dinenage